FLAVORS
of
HOME

Creative Cooking
from Down-Home to Gourmet

Patti Shenfield

Front Cover
Old-Fashioned Tomato Macaroni Soup, page 62
Cornish Pasties, page 125

Flavors of Home
by
Patti Shenfield

First Printing — February 1994

Published by
Palastair Enterprises
P.O. Box 5082
Drayton Valley, Alberta
T0E 0M0

Canadian Cataloguing in Publication Data
Shenfield, Patti, 1957-
  Flavors of home
  Includes index.
  ISBN 1-895292-37-9

1. Cookery. I. Title.

TX714.S54 1994   641.5   C94-920056-5

Photography by:
Merle Prosofsky
Merle Prosofsky Photography
Edmonton, Alberta

Dishes and Accessories Compliments of:
Eaton's
Blais Home Hardware

Designed, Printed and Produced in Canada by:
Centax Books, a Division of PrintWest Communications Ltd.
Publishing Director, Photo Designer & Food Stylist: Margo Embury
1150 Eighth Avenue, Regina, Saskatchewan, Canada S4R 1C9
(306) 525-2304 FAX: (306) 757-2439

Table of Contents

Most of these recipes are made from fresh natural ingredients. However, seasoning powders are added in some recipes to intensify the flavors. As a practical convenience to busy cooks, some recipes use prepared sauces or soups. Often "scratch" variations are provided but most of us today appreciate the time-saving convenience of using commercial, prepared products as shortcuts in our home cooking.

Recipes have been tested in U.S. Standard measurements. Common metric measurements are given as a convenience for those who are more familiar with metric. Recipes have not been tested in metric.

Introduction

Patti Shenfield grew up in the Edmonton, Alberta area. From the age of ten, she has been creating her own recipes and adapting the favorite recipes of family members and friends, using "on-hand" ingredients found in most kitchen cupboards. Patti started out making birthday cakes with a friend and her interest in cooking developed from there. Her mother let her have free reign of the kitchen to experiment as she pleased.

Patti has lived all over Alberta and has done some travelling around the world where she has exchanged many recipes with friends. This is a collection of her best dishes.

Patti now resides in Drayton Valley, Alberta where her husband, Butch, and four children test and sample her creations. She works part-time as a cook at a Senior Citizens lodge where she serves some of her more traditional recipes to the residents.

In *Flavors of Home* you will find many new and interesting flavor combinations as well as old standbys. This book will please the palate of young and old alike with its wide range of traditional classics and contemporary favorites. Enjoy the recipes from *Flavors of Home* at your next gathering, whether it be a family reunion or quiet meal for four.

Variations are a special feature of this book. Many of the recipes suggest alternate ingredients to suit taste preferences, special occasions or convenience. These variations help beginning cooks develop their own creativity and encourage all cooks to produce their own *Flavors of Home*.

Thank You

This book is dedicated to my husband, Butch, and my children, Jennifer, Stephen, James and Robyn, who helped in so many ways, and to other family members for filling roles from tasters to typists to financiers and for putting up with my papers and references scattered over and around the dining room table for the last few years.

My special thanks goes to those many people who gave me the encouragement to continue my pursuit of putting this book together, and for those who gave me permission to add their favorite recipes to mine. Your favorites became my favorites but credit remains with you. Thank you for bringing these flavors to so many homes.

Breakfasts, Muffins & Breads

Hearty Sausage Omelet

This makes a satisfying one-dish breakfast.

½ lb.	bulk pork sausage	250 g
¼ cup	chopped onion	60 mL
¼ cup	chopped green pepper	60 mL
12 oz.	frozen hash-brown potatoes (3 cups [750 mL])	340 g
4	eggs	4
¼ cup	milk	60 mL
½ cup	grated Cheddar cheese	125 mL
	salt and pepper to taste	

- In a deep skillet, brown sausage and remove from pan. Drain off fat and reserve ¼ cup (60 mL) drippings.
- Cook onions, peppers and hash-brown potatoes in drippings until hash browns are golden brown and onions and peppers are tender.
- Beat eggs and milk and pour over potato mixture. Reduce heat to low.
- Sprinkle sausage and cheese over potato and egg mixture. Cover and cook over low heat for 10-15 minutes, or until eggs are set. Loosen from bottom of skillet with metal spatula.
- Cut into wedges and serve with toast.

Serves 8.

Variations: *This can also be baked in the oven. Place cooked meat, hash browns, onion and green pepper in a greased 9-10" (23-25 cm) pie plate. Pour egg mixture over and sprinkle with cheese. Bake at 325°F (160°C) for 25-30 minutes, or until eggs are set.*

To make Hearty Ham Omelet, substitute ½ lb. (250 g) of cubed ham for sausage.

Homemade Sausage

1 lb.	fresh ground pork	500 g
¼ tsp.	Worcestershire sauce	1 mL
½ tsp.	onion powder	2 mL
¼ tsp.	dried sage	1 mL
	salt and pepper to taste	

- Combine all ingredients and fry as for bulk pork sausage. This is also good made into miniature meatballs for minestrone soup.

Ham and Cheese Strata

This is a terrific brunch entrée.

6	slices bread, crusts removed	6
1 lb.	precooked ham in ½" (1.3 cm) cubes	500g
½ lb.	Cheddar cheese, cubed OR grated	250 g
8	eggs, beaten	8
2 cups	milk	500 mL
½ tsp.	dry mustard	2 mL
½ tsp.	Worcestershire sauce	2 mL
¼ cup	butter OR margarine, melted	60 mL
1 tbsp.	chopped chives OR green onion	15 mL
½ cup	broken cornflakes (optional)	125 mL

- Butter a 9 x 13" (23 x 33 cm) baking pan.
- Tear bread into pieces and spread over bottom of pan.
- Scatter ham and cheese cubes over bread pieces.
- Beat eggs and add milk, dry mustard and Worcestershire sauce.
- Pour egg mixture over bread, ham and cheese.
- Pour melted butter over all and sprinkle with chives.
- Cover with plastic wrap and refrigerate overnight.
- Remove from refrigerator and sprinkle with cornflakes.
- Bake, uncovered, at 325°F (160°C) for 1 hour.
- Serve with fruit and toast for breakfast or with salad for a luncheon.

Serves 8.

Substitutions:

1 tbsp. (15 mL) cornstarch	= 2 tbsp. (30 mL) flour (for thickening only)
1 cup buttermilk or sour milk	= 1 cup (250 mL) milk plus 1 tbsp. (15 mL) vinegar or lemon juice (let stand at room temperature for 5 minutes)
1 square (1 oz. [30 g]) unsweetened chocolate	= 3 tbsp. (45 mL) cocoa plus 1 tbsp. (15 mL) butter or margarine.
Beef Broth	= 1 cup (250 mL) hot water plus 1 tsp. (5 mL) instant beef granules or 1 bouillon cube
Chicken Broth	= same as above only use instant chicken granules or chicken bouillon cube
Yogurt	= sour cream
Sour Cream, 35% (whipping) cream, mayonnaise	= For a low-fat or no-fat version, combine equal amounts of low-fat or no-fat cottage cheese and no-fat or low-fat yogurt and purée in blender. Note: This product will not whip.

Breakfast Sandwiches

A delicious and nutritious breakfast sandwich, also a great late-night snack.

3	strips bacon	3
2	slices bread	2
1	egg	1
	butter	
	salt and pepper to taste	
1	cheese slice	1
2	slices fresh tomato	2
	mayonnaise	

- Fry bacon, drain on paper towel and keep warm.
- Toast and butter 2 pieces of bread.
- Lightly whisk 1 egg and fry in a small amount of butter. Sprinkle with salt and pepper, turn egg over and place a slice of cheese on egg.
- Place egg and cheese on 1 piece of buttered toast. Top with bacon and tomato.
- Spread some mayonnaise on other piece of buttered toast; place over tomato.

Makes 1 sandwich, increase amounts as needed.

Equivalent Amounts:

Apples	- 1 apple	= 1 cup (250 mL) chopped
	- 1 pound	= 2¾ cups (675 mL) sliced
Bananas	- 3 medium, mashed	= 1 cup (250 mL)
Bread crumbs	- 1½ fresh slices	= 1 cup (250 mL) soft crumbs
	- 4 slices dry bread	= 1 cup (250 mL) fine crumbs
Butter/margarine	- 1 ounce (30 g)	= 2 tbsp. (30 mL)
Carrots	- 1 pound (500 g)	= 7 medium = 3 cups (750 mL) grated
Celery	- 1 stalk, sliced	= ½ cup (125 mL)
Cheddar cheese	- 4 ounces (115 g)	= 1 cup (250 mL) grated
Chocolate	- 1 ounce (30 g)	= 1 square = ¼ cup (60 mL) chocolate chips
Garlic	- 1 clove	= ⅛ tsp. (0.5 mL) garlic powder
Graham wafers	- 14 wafers, crushed	= 1 cup (250 mL) crumbs
Herbs	- 1 tbsp. (15 mL) fresh	= 1 tsp. (5 mL) dry
Lemons	- 1 medium	= 3 tbsp. (45 mL) juice
Macaroni	- 4 ounces (115 g)	= 1 cup (250 mL) dry
		= 2 cups (500 mL) cooked
Mushrooms	- ¼ pound (115 g)	= 1¼ cups (300 mL) sliced
Onions	- 1 medium	= ½ cup (125 mL) chopped
	- 1 small	= 1 tbsp. (15 mL) instant onion flakes
Rice, long-grain	- 1 cup (250 mL) dry	= 3 cups (750 mL) cooked
Soda crackers	- 28 crackers, crushed	= 1 cup (250 mL) crumbs
Vanilla wafers	- 22 wafers, crushed	= 1 cup (250 mL) crumbs
Whipping cream	- 1 cup (250 mL) cream	= 2 cups (500 mL) whipped

Basic Crêpes

Crêpes in all their lovely variations are perfect for a special breakfast, brunch, lunch, dinner or even a midnight supper. Enjoy these delicate morsels in all of the sweet and savory variations.

3	eggs	3
1 cup	milk	250 mL
1 tbsp.	sugar	15 mL
3 tbsp.	melted butter OR margarine OR oil	45 mL
½ tsp.	salt	2 mL
¾ cup	flour	175 mL

- Pour all ingredients into a blender or mixing bowl and blend until smooth.
- Scrape sides and beat again.
- Refrigerate for 1 hour.
- Take about 3 tbsp. (45 mL) of batter and pour onto a greased hot crêpe pan or skillet. Spread to about a 6" (15 cm) diameter. Cook over medium-high heat until lightly browned on bottom and top is not doughy.
- Loosen edges and invert on a plate.

Yield: 12 crêpes.

Note: *The first crêpe usually doesn't look great but the following crêpes will be nice. Fill with your favorite fillings and roll up.*

Crêpes can be made ahead and frozen for a later date. Do not freeze with fillings inside. Place waxed paper between each crêpe before freezing, then cover stack of crêpes with plastic wrap.

Strawberry Crêpes

	ice cream	
	prepared crêpes, above	
1 cup	whipping cream, whipped	250 mL
16 oz.	pkg. frozen sliced strawberries in syrup, thawed	500 g

- Slice ice cream into 1 x 1 x 5" (2.5 x 2.5 x 13 cm) sticks and place each on a crêpe or spoon ice cream in a strip down center of crêpe. Roll up crêpes.
- Spoon whipping cream and strawberries over top.

Peaches and Cream Crêpes

3	peaches, peeled and sliced	3
¼ cup	water	60 mL
⅓ cup	sugar	75 mL
1 tbsp.	cornstarch	15 mL
1 cup	whipping cream, whipped	250 mL
	prepared crêpes, page 9	

- In a small saucepan, place peaches and 2 tbsp. (30 mL) of water.
- Simmer until peaches are tender, about 5 minutes.
- Add sugar and stir.
- Combine cornstarch and remaining water. Stir until cornstarch is dissolved. Stir into peach mixture and cook until thick. Cool.
- Roll filling in crêpes and top with whipped cream.

Variation: *Canned peaches may be used. Use ¼ cup (60 mL) peach juice from can instead of the ¼ cup (60 mL) water.*

Banana Crêpes

prepared crêpes, page 9
bananas, halved lengthwise
chocolate sauce
whipping cream, whipped
chopped peanuts

- Roll a crêpe around a banana half.
- Drizzle chocolate sauce on top.
- Add dollops of whipped cream.
- Sprinkle with peanuts.

Beef Stroganoff Crêpes

- Prepare Chinese Beef with Broccoli, page 111, but omit the broccoli. Add ½ cup (125 mL) sour cream to gravy. Fill and roll prepared crêpes.
- If crêpes are warm and filling is piping hot, it is not necessary to bake crêpes. Serve them at once. If crêpes are filled and assembled ahead, place filled crêpes in a single layer in a shallow pan. Cover with sauce or gravy and bake at 400°F (200°C) for 10-15 minutes, until bubbling and lightly browned.

Chicken À La King Crêpes

- Prepare Chicken à la King, page 100. Fill and roll prepared crêpes. See serving and baking instructions above.

Ham and Egg Crêpes

eggs
cubed ham
prepared crêpes
Hollandaise OR cheese sauce

- Scramble eggs with cubed ham. Fill and roll prepared crêpes. Drizzle with your favorite Hollandaise sauce or cheese sauce. See serving and baking instructions above.

Chicken Tarragon Crêpes

2 cups	chicken broth	500 mL
½ tsp.	dry tarragon flakes	2 mL
¼ tsp.	cumin	1 mL
¼ tsp.	soy sauce	1 mL
1 cup	milk	250 mL
¼ cup	cornstarch	60 mL
3 cups	chopped cooked chicken	750 mL
	prepared crêpes	

- In a medium saucepan, heat broth, tarragon and cumin. Simmer 3 minutes.
- Add soy sauce.
- Mix milk and cornstarch together until cornstarch dissolves. Add to broth and stir over medium heat until thick. Stir in chicken and warm through. Fill and roll prepared crêpes. See serving and baking instructions above.

Pancakes

Light, fluffy and moist.

2 cups	flour	500 mL
3 tbsp.	sugar	45 mL
2 tbsp.	baking powder (Yes! 2 tbsp. [30 mL])	30 mL
½ tsp.	salt	2 mL
2	eggs	2
2 cups	milk	500 mL
2 tbsp.	oil	30 mL

- In a large mixing bowl, combine flour, sugar, baking powder and salt. Mix well.
- Make a well in the middle of the dry ingredients in the bowl. Set aside.
- Whisk together eggs, milk and oil.
- Pour egg mixture in well in dry ingredients. Stir until you have a thick batter.
- Pour batter in ¼ cup (60 mL) portions on a hot, lightly oiled griddle. You should have to oil griddle only once.
- Flip pancakes when bubbles appear on top and the bottom is golden brown.
- Serve with butter and syrup or your favorite toppings.

Yield: 16 medium-sized pancakes.

Variations:

Banana Pancakes: *Add 1 puréed banana to wet ingredients.*

Blueberry Pancakes: *Sprinkle blueberries on pancake batter after it is poured on the griddle. This prevents "blue batter".*

Your Favorites: *Try adding drained corn niblets, grated apple, chopped peaches, grated cheese, etc. to the batter. Use your imagination and enjoy a creative brunch.*

Cornmeal Pancakes: *Add ¼ cup (60 mL) cornmeal and ¼ cup (60 mL) more milk.*

Crispy Waffles

2¼ cups	flour	550 mL
2 tbsp.	baking powder (Yes! 2 tbsp. [30 mL])	30 mL
2 tbsp.	sugar	30 mL
½ tsp.	salt	2 mL
2	eggs, separated	2
2¼ cups	milk	550 mL
½ cup	oil	125 mL

- In a large mixing bowl, combine flour, sugar, baking powder and salt. Whisk until evenly mixed. Make a well in dry ingredients and set aside.
- Beat egg yolks, milk and oil. Add to well in dry ingredients and beat until moistened.
- Beat egg whites until stiff and fold into batter, leaving tiny clouds of egg white throughout batter.
- Pour onto an oiled, preheated waffle iron. Bake about 4 minutes, until the waffle releases when the top of the waffle iron is raised.
- Serve with butter and your favorite toppings. Try syrups, fresh fruit or the sauces on page 14.

Yield: 8-10 waffles.

Variations:

Banana Waffles: *Add one puréed banana to wet ingredients.*

Blueberry Waffles: *Sprinkle blueberries over batter after spooning onto waffle iron.*

Your Favorites: *Try adding 1 cup (250 mL) puréed apricots or peaches or drained crushed pineapple. For orange-flavored waffles, try substituting half the milk with orange juice and add 2 tbsp. (30 mL) finely grated orange rind. Up to 1 cup (250 mL) of chopped nuts and/or raisins could also be added to waffle batter.*

Pancake and Waffle Toppings

Blueberry Sauce

2 cups	blueberries, fresh OR frozen	500 mL
¾ cup	sugar	175 mL
1 tbsp.	cornstarch	15 mL
⅛ tsp.	cinnamon	0.5 mL

- Place blueberries in a small saucepan.
- Mix sugar and cornstarch together and pour over blueberries.
- Cook over medium heat until thick and bubbly, and until cornstarch taste is gone. You may add water to thin the sauce to the desired consistency.

Apricot Sauce

14 oz.	can apricot halves	398 mL
¼ tsp.	cinnamon	1 mL
2 tbsp.	butter	30 mL
	whipped cream (optional)	

- Drain apricots and reserve ½ of the syrup.
- In a small saucepan, place apricots, reserved syrup, cinnamon and butter.
- Cook over medium heat until thick and bubbly.
- Serve warm over waffles or pancakes. A dollop of whipped cream on top really brings out the flavor.

Strawberry Sauce

16 oz.	pkg. frozen sliced strawberries, thawed	500 g
1 tbsp.	cornstarch	15 mL
	whipped cream	

- Pour strawberries into a small saucepan. Stir in cornstarch and mix well.
- Cook over medium heat until thickened.
- Serve warm or cold with a dollop of whipped cream.

Homemade Flour Tortillas

These are simple to make and so nice to eat with your favorite Mexican dishes. Included in this book are several recipes which use these tortillas. You may make them ahead and freeze them before you cook them or after they are cooked. (Separate with waxed paper.)

5 cups	flour	1.25 L
2 tbsp.	baking powder	30 mL
2 tsp.	salt	10 mL
1 cup	shortening	250 mL
1¾ cups	cold water	425 mL

- Combine dry ingredients.
- Cut or rub shortening into dry ingredients until mixture is coarse.
- Add water a bit at a time, mixing well, until you have to mix with your hands.
- Divide the dough into 12 pieces and leave in a bowl covered with a wet towel while working.
- Roll a piece of dough into a ball; then place on a generously floured surface.
- Roll out quite thin with a rolling pin. Turn once while rolling to make sure the surfaces are well floured. (If you want perfectly round circles place a dinner plate on rolled out dough and trim around the plate.)
- To cook tortillas, heat your griddle to a fairly high heat, 375-400°F (190-200°C). Lightly grease the griddle (you need not use oil or grease on a non-stick surface).
- Cook the tortillas until you see bubbles appear on the surface, then check with a spatula underneath to see if there are slightly browned spots. Turn and cook the other side the same way. (Do not leave tortillas unattended on the griddle, as they burn easily at this high heat and can get hard and unbendable which can be frustrating to a little child (or a big one) when they take their first bite.

Yield: 12 large tortillas.

Note: *These tortillas cook very fast. It doesn't take long to bake a dozen. Homemade tortillas are more pastry-like and not quite as thick and chewy as those you buy at the store. These tortillas shrink as they fry.*

Variation: *To make taco shells, place tortilla in 1" (2.5 cm) of hot oil in an electric frying pan or any other type of heavy deep skillet. Use a pair of tongs and fold over holding one edge 2-3" (5-7.5 cm) above the other edge. When crisp and lightly browned on 1 side, flip over and do the same on the other side. Drain on paper toweling and keep warm.*

English Scones

1¾ cups	flour	425 mL
¼ cup	sugar	60 mL
1 tbsp.	baking powder	15 mL
½ tsp.	salt	2 mL
½ cup	currants OR raisins	125 mL
⅓ cup	butter OR margarine	75 mL
1	egg	1
⅓ cup	milk OR cereal cream	75 mL
1	egg, beaten (for glazing)	1

- Preheat oven to 400°F (200°C).
- In a medium-sized bowl, combine flour, sugar, baking powder and salt. Stir in currants.
- Rub or cut butter into flour until mixture resembles coarse crumbs.
- Beat egg and stir in cream. Pour into dry ingredients and stir until you have a soft dough.
- On a lightly floured surface, knead lightly until mixed, about 8-10 times.
- Roll ½" (1.3 cm) thick and cut with a round cutter or a standard Mason jar lid.
- Place on an ungreased cookie sheet.
- Brush tops with beaten egg.
- Bake for 10-12 minutes, or until golden brown.
- Serve with butter, jam, jelly or honey.

Yield: 10-12 scones.

Variation: *Dough can be pressed into a 9" (23 cm) greased pie plate and baked about 15 minutes, or until a toothpick comes out clean. Cut into wedges.*

Breakfast

Prize-Winning Danish Pastries, page 28

Flaky Buttermilk Biscuits

Such a light and flaky biscuit — perfect with honey or jam.

2 cups	flour	500 mL
4 tsp.	baking powder	20 mL
1/4 tsp.	baking soda	1 mL
1/2 tsp.	cream of tartar	2 mL
1/2 tsp.	salt	2 mL
1 tbsp.	sugar	15 mL
1/2 cup	shortening OR margarine	125 mL
1	egg	1
2/3 cup	buttermilk	150 mL

- Preheat oven to 425°F (220°C).
- Place all dry ingredients in a large mixing bowl. Stir to blend.
- Cut or rub in shortening until the size of peas and the mixture resembles coarse meal.
- Make a well in the center of the dry ingredients.
- Mix egg and buttermilk together and add to well in dry ingredients.
- Mix until dough is moistened and forms a ball.
- Roll out 3/4" (2 cm) thick on a floured surface. Use a lot of flour for rolling because dough is very sticky.
- Cut with a round cookie cutter and place biscuits on a lightly greased baking sheet.
- Bake for 10-12 minutes, or until golden brown.

Yield: 12 biscuits.

Variations: *Regular milk can be substituted for buttermilk.*

Herbed Biscuits: *Add 1-2 tbsp. (15-30 mL) of chopped dried herbs OR 2-4 tbsp. (30-60 mL) of chopped fresh herbs to dry ingredients. Use about half parsley and add your choice of basil, oregano, thyme and/or sage.*

Onion Garlic Biscuits: *To Herbed Biscuits add 1/4 cup (60 mL) minced onion and 1-2 garlic cloves, crushed, plus 1/8 tsp. (0.5 mL) of hot pepper sauce or cayenne pepper.*

Cheesy Biscuits: *Add 1/2 cup (125 mL) or more of very strong, finely grated Cheddar and a sprinkle or two of cayenne pepper.*

Hint: *Use a standard Mason jar lid as a biscuit cutter.*

Yorkshire Pudding

The puffiest Yorkshires you'll ever make.

¼ cup	shortening	60 mL
4	eggs	4
1¾ cups	milk	425 mL
1 cup	flour	250 mL
¼ tsp.	salt	1 mL

- Preheat oven to 425°F (220°C).
- Lightly grease sides of 12 muffin cups with nonstick spray.
- Place 1 tsp. (5 mL) shortening into each of 12 muffin cups (don't spread around). Set aside.
- In a medium bowl, combine eggs and milk. Beat until smooth. Beat in flour and salt. Beat again until smooth.
- Place muffin tin in oven until shortening is melted and starts to smoke.
- Remove pan from oven.
- Immediately pour batter into hot muffin cups.
- Return to oven and bake for 20 minutes.
- Serve with roast beef and gravy for an elegant, satisfying meal.

Yield: 12 large Yorkshires.

Variations:

Popovers: *Popovers are a wonderful breakfast treat. They are very similar to Yorkshire Pudding. Using the above batter, grease bottoms and sides of muffin cups with nonstick spray or shortening and dust with flour, sugar or grated Parmesan cheese. Prepare batter as above (omitting steps 5 and 6) and pour into muffin cups. Bake at 450°F (230°C) for 15 minutes. Reduce heat to 350°F (180°C) and bake for 20 minutes, until sides are firm. Serve with butter and apricot, strawberry or your favorite jam.*

Lemon Poppy Seed Muffins

2 cups	flour	500 mL
1 tsp.	baking soda	5 mL
1 tsp.	baking powder	5 mL
1 tbsp.	poppy seeds	15 mL
½ cup	sugar	125 mL
¼ tsp.	salt	1 mL
¼ cup	butter OR margarine, melted	60 mL
1 cup	plain yogurt	250 mL
1	egg	1
¼ cup	lemon juice	60 mL
½ tsp.	grated lemon rind	2 mL

Glaze:

2 tbsp.	sugar	30 mL
1 tbsp.	lemon juice	15 mL

- Preheat oven to 375°F (190°C).
- In a large bowl, combine flour, baking soda, baking powder, poppy seeds, sugar and salt. Make a well in the center and set aside.
- In a small bowl, mix melted butter, yogurt, egg, lemon juice and rind. Whisk until smooth.
- Pour wet ingredients into the well in dry ingredients and stir until moistened. DO NOT OVERMIX.
- Spoon into 12 well-greased muffin cups.
- Bake for 20-25 minutes.
- Remove from oven and set on cooling racks.
- Combine glaze ingredients and brush muffins with glaze while still in pans.

Yield: 12 medium muffins.

Blueberry Muffins

After picking blueberries, reward yourself by making these heavenly muffins.

⅔ cup	butter OR margarine	150 mL
⅔ cup	sugar	150 mL
2	eggs	2
1½ tsp.	vanilla	7 mL
2⅓ cups	all-purpose flour	575 mL
2 tbsp.	baking powder	30 mL
½ tsp.	cinnamon	2 mL
½ tsp.	salt	2 mL
1⅓ cups	milk	325 mL
1½ cups	blueberries	375 mL
	Streusel Topping, page 23, (optional)	

- Preheat oven to 350°F (180°C).
- In a large mixing bowl, cream butter and sugar. Add eggs and vanilla and beat until light and fluffy.
- In a small bowl, combine flour, baking powder, cinnamon and salt.
- Add the flour mixture to the egg mixture alternately with the milk. After each addition, stir until everything is mixed.
- DO NOT OVER MIX.
- Fold in blueberries.
- Pour into 18 or 24 greased muffin cups.
- Top with Streusel Topping, if using.
- Bake for 20-25 minutes.

Yield: 24 medium muffins OR 18 large muffins.

Variation:

Peach Muffins: *Substitute coarsely chopped, fresh or canned peaches for blueberries.*

22

Apple Muffins

These are good anytime, but are best served warm.

4 cups	peeled and shredded apples	1 L
1 cup	sugar	250 mL
2	eggs, lightly beaten	2
½ cup	butter OR margarine, melted	125 mL
2 tsp.	vanilla	10 mL
1½ cups	all-purpose flour	375 mL
½ cup	whole-wheat flour (can use all white flour)	125 mL
2 tsp.	baking soda	10 mL
1 tsp.	cinnamon	5 mL
¼ tsp.	nutmeg	1 mL
1 tsp.	salt	5 mL
1 cup	broken OR chopped walnuts (optional)	250 mL
1 cup	raisins	250 mL

- Preheat oven to 350°F (180°C).
- In a large mixing bowl, combine shredded apples and sugar.
- In another bowl, combine eggs, butter and vanilla. Stir to blend.
- In another bowl, combine flours, baking soda, spices and salt. Mix well.
- Stir egg mixture into apple mixture. Stir in dry ingredients until moistened.
- Stir in nuts and raisins.
- Spoon batter into 18 greased muffin cups.
- Top with streusel topping (below), if desired.
- Bake for 15-20 minutes, or until a toothpick inserted in the center comes out clean.

Yield: 18 large muffins.

Streusel Topping

⅓ cup	brown sugar	75 mL
⅓ cup	chopped nuts	75 mL
½ tsp.	cinnamon	2 mL

- Combine all ingredients.
- Sprinkle a spoonful of topping on each muffin before baking.

Note: This topping is also good on blueberry muffins.

Cinnamon Carrot Muffins

A moist basic recipe that can also be baked as a loaf.

1 cup	sugar	250 mL
³⁄₄ cup	oil	175 mL
2	eggs	2
1 cup	finely grated carrots	250 mL
1²⁄₃ cups	flour	400 mL
1 tsp.	baking powder	5 mL
1 tsp.	baking soda	5 mL
1 tsp.	cinnamon	5 mL
½ tsp.	salt	2 mL
½ cup	chopped walnuts	125 mL
½ cup	raisins (optional)	125 mL

- Preheat oven to 350°F (180°C).
- In a large mixing bowl, beat sugar, oil and eggs together until light.
- With a spoon, stir in carrots.
- In another bowl, combine flour, baking powder, baking soda, spices, salt, nuts and raisins, if using.
- Make a hole in the center of the dry ingredients.
- Pour egg mixture into the hole.
- Mix until dry ingredients are just moistened.
- Pour into 12 greased muffin cups.
- Bake for 20 minutes, or until a toothpick comes out clean.

Yield: **12 large muffins.**

Variations:

Carrot Bran Muffins: *Add ²⁄₃ cup (150 mL) bran.*

Carrot Loaf: *Mix batter as above and pour into a 5 x 9" (13 x 23 cm) loaf pan. Bake at 325°F (160°C) for 1 hour, or until a toothpick comes out clean.*

Spicy Pumpkin Muffins

These give off a wonderful spicy aroma while baking.

½ cup	butter OR margarine	125 mL
1 cup	sugar	250 mL
2	eggs	2
¾ cup	pumpkin purée	175 mL
1¾ cups	flour	425 mL
1 tsp.	baking soda	5 mL
1 tsp.	cinnamon	5 mL
½ tsp.	salt	2 mL
¼ tsp.	ginger	1 mL
¼ tsp.	allspice	1 mL
¼ tsp.	mace	1 mL
½ cup	chopped walnuts	125 mL

- Preheat oven to 350°F (180°C).
- In a large mixing bowl, cream together butter and sugar.
- Add eggs and beat until light and fluffy.
- Add pumpkin and beat until well mixed.
- Combine flour, baking soda and spices.
- Stir dry ingredients into pumpkin mixture until moistened.
- DO NOT OVER STIR OR YOU WILL GET PEAKS AND TUNNELS IN YOUR MUFFINS.
- Stir in nuts.
- Spoon into 12 greased large muffin cups.
- Bake for 20 minutes, or until a toothpick inserted in middle comes out clean.

Yield: 12 large muffins.

Variations: *These are nice frosted with Cream Cheese Frosting, page 155, or Mock Cream Cheese Frosting, page 153. For a sweeter muffin, add ¼ cup (60 mL) more sugar.*

Healthy Pumpkin Muffins

This recipe was created by my sister Janelle who is very "health conscious".

4	eggs	4
1 cup	sugar	250 mL
1½ cups	oil	375 mL
14 oz.	can pumpkin purée	398 mL
2 cups	all-purpose flour	500 mL
1 cup	whole-wheat flour	250 mL
¼ cup	wheat germ	60 mL
¼ cup	oat bran	60 mL
1 tbsp.	cinnamon	15 mL
2 tsp.	baking soda	10 mL
1 tsp.	salt	5 mL
2 tsp.	baking powder	10 mL
½ cup	raisins	125 mL
½ cup	chopped pecans OR walnuts	125 mL
½ cup	Granola, page 190, OR rolled oats for topping	125 mL

- Preheat oven to 350°F (180°C).
- In a small bowl, beat eggs, sugar, oil and pumpkin until well mixed. Set aside.
- In a large mixing bowl, combine remaining ingredients, except granola or oats.
- Make a well in the middle of the dry ingredients.
- Pour liquid mixture into well in dry ingredients and stir to moisten.
- Fill 24 greased or paper-lined muffin cups to the top. Sprinkle with granola or oats.
- Bake for 20 minutes, or until a toothpick inserted in center comes out clean.

Yield: 24 large muffins.

Variations: *½ cup (125 mL) rolled oats may be substituted for the ¼ cup (60 mL) wheat germ and ¼ cup (60 mL) oat bran.*

½ cup (125 mL) applesauce may be substituted for ½ cup (125 mL) of the oil.

1 cup (250 mL) all-purpose flour may be substituted for 1 cup (250 mL) of whole-wheat flour.

Cinnamon Rolls

These will bring back childhood memories when they are fresh from the oven.

2 cups	warm water	500 mL
¼ cup	honey	60 mL
2 tbsp.	yeast	30 mL
¼ cup	butter OR margarine, melted	60 mL
1 tsp.	salt	5 mL
2	eggs	2
1 tbsp.	lemon juice	15 mL
½ cup	raisins	125 mL
5-6 cups	flour	1.25-1.5 L
½ cup	butter OR margarine	125 mL
1½ cups	brown sugar	375 mL
2 tbsp.	cinnamon	30 mL
	Bun Icing, page 29	

- In a large mixing bowl, combine water, honey and yeast; let stand 10 minutes.
- Add melted butter, salt, eggs and lemon juice. Beat until frothy.
- Add raisins and half of the flour. Beat until smooth. Stir in remaining flour, 1 cup (250 mL) at a time, until dough is smooth but stiff.
- Knead in flour that cannot be stirred in. Knead until smooth and elastic but not sticky.
- Turn into a greased bowl and let rise until double in bulk. Punch down.
- Divide into 2 pieces and roll each piece into a 12" (30 cm) square.
- Spread with butter.
- Mix brown sugar and cinnamon together. Sprinkle over butter and roll up like a jelly roll, sealing the edges.
- Slice in 1" (2.5 cm) pieces with a thread, dental floss or a sharp knife.
- Place each piece in a 9 x 13" (23 x 33 cm) pan, greased with butter and sprinkled liberally with brown sugar.
- Let rise in a warm place until double in bulk.
- Bake at 350°F (180°C) for 20-25 minutes.
- Invert on a cooling rack.
- When cooler but still a bit warm turn over and drizzle Bun Icing, page 29, over top.

Yield: 24 buns.

Variation:

Caramel Rolls: *After placing unbaked rolls in pan, pour ⅓ cup (75 mL) cream or evaporated milk evenly over buns. Let rise; bake as above.*

Prize-Winning Danish Pastries

This recipe makes fabulous Danish Pastries or Croissants.

2½ cups	COLD milk	625 mL
1 tsp.	sugar	5 mL
2 tbsp.	yeast	30 mL
¼ cup	sugar	60 mL
2	large eggs	2
2 tsp.	salt	10 mL
2 tbsp.	butter OR margarine	30 mL
6 cups	flour (approximately)	1.5 L
1 cup	butter OR margarine (Do not add to dough!)	250 mL
1	egg	1
2 tbsp.	milk	30 mL
	apricot jam	
	warm water	

- Warm ½ cup (125 mL) of the milk and add 1 tsp. (5 mL) sugar and the yeast.
- Soften for 7 minutes then refrigerate until cold. It is important that Danish Pastry dough is cold!
- In a large mixing bowl, mix 2 cups (500 mL) cold milk, cold yeast mixture, sugar, eggs, salt, 2 tbsp. (30 mL) butter and 1 cup (250 ml) of flour.
- Beat until smooth.
- Stir in 3 more cups (750 mL) of flour, 1 cup (250 mL) at a time.
- Knead in remaining flour until you have a smooth elastic dough. This dough should be soft, not too firm.
- Place dough, covered, on a floured surface and let rest for 30 minutes.
- Punch dough down and knead for 1 minute.
- On a floured surface, roll dough into a 12 x 24" (30 x 60 cm) rectangle. Brush off any flour on surface of dough.
- With a knife, teaspoon or your fingers, dot margarine onto ⅔ of the dough's surface (12 x 16" [30 x 41 cm]). Make sure that the ⅔ is covered evenly.
- Fold the plain ⅓ over half of the buttered side (see diagram page 29), then fold the remaining side over the plain side. Make sure you brush off any flour on surface.
- Place dough on a floured 10 x 15" (25 x 38 cm) jelly roll pan.
- Refrigerate for 20 minutes.
- Remove from refrigerator and place on a lightly floured surface.
- Roll to a 12 x 24" (30 x 60 cm) rectangle again. Fold in thirds again, making sure you dust off any flour from dough's surface while folding.
- Chill for 20 minutes.

Prize-Winning Danish Pastries

Continued

- Repeat the folding procedure 2 more times.
- After the last folding, place dough on jelly roll pan, cover with plastic wrap and chill 3 hours or overnight.
- Remove dough from refrigerator.
- Place dough on a cool surface; roll dough to a 16 x 24" (41 x 60 cm) rectangle.
- Cut strips 16" (41 cm) long x ¾" (2 cm) wide. Twist each strip like a party streamer and roll strips in a flat spiral on a greased 10 x 15" (25 x 38 cm) pan. They should look like snails.
- Brush lightly with an eggwash made with 1 egg and 2 tbsp. (30 mL) of milk whisked together.
- Set pan in a warm place to rise for about 45 minutes, or until double in bulk.
- Preheat oven to 350°F (180°C).
- When risen, make an indentation in the middle of each Danish and fill with a teaspoonful (5 mL) of filling, see pages 30 and 31.
- Bake for 20 minutes, or until golden brown.
- Remove from oven and place on cooling racks.
- Dilute apricot jam with warm water to make a syrup. Glaze warm buns with apricot syrup.
- Then drizzle bun icing (below) over pastries.

Yield: 36 Danish pastries OR 32 croissants.

See photograph on page 17.

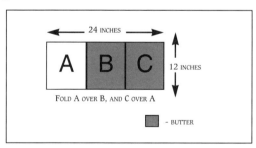

Bun Icing

¼ cup	cold water	60 mL
1¾ cups	icing sugar	425 mL
¼ tsp.	lemon extract	1 mL

- Place all ingredients in a small bowl and beat until smooth, then drizzle over Danish pastries.

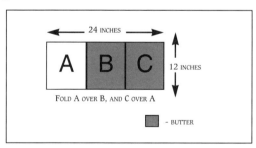

Bavarian Cream Danish Filling

1 tbsp.	cornstarch	15 mL
¼ cup	cold evaporated milk	60 mL
1 cup	scalded milk	250 mL
2 tbsp.	sugar	30 mL
2	egg yolks, beaten	2
⅛ tsp.	salt	0.5 mL
½ tsp.	vanilla	2 mL

- Dissolve cornstarch in the cold evaporated milk.
- Add scalded milk to egg yolks in a double boiler over simmering water.
- Add salt and cornstarch mixture. Cook until it coats a metal spoon.
- Remove from heat. Stir in vanilla. Cool.

Yield: 1½ cups (375 mL).

Apple Danish Filling

2	medium apples peeled, cored and diced (1¾ cups [425 mL])	2
¼ cup	water	60 mL
⅛ tsp.	salt	0.5 mL
2 tbsp.	sugar	30 mL
¼ tsp.	cinnamon	1 mL
1 tbsp.	cornstarch	15 mL
2 tbsp.	cold water	30 mL

- In a small saucepan, combine apples, ¼ cup (60 mL) water and salt, and bring to a boil.
- Simmer over medium heat for 3 minutes, or until apples are tender.
- Add sugar and cinnamon. Stir over medium heat until sugar dissolves.
- Combine cornstarch and 2 tbsp. (30 mL) of cold water. Stir into apple mixture.
- Cook until thickened; remove from heat and cool.

Yield: 1¼ cups (300 mL).

Variation:
Peach Filling: *Substitute peaches for apples and add 2 tsp. (10 mL) more cornstarch.*

Lemon Danish Filling

³/₄ cup	cold water	175 mL
¼ cup	lemon juice	60 mL
½ cup	sugar	125 mL
2 tbsp.	cornstarch	30 mL
1	egg yolk	1
½ tsp.	lemon extract	2 mL
1 tbsp.	butter	15 mL
4	drops yellow food coloring	4

- In the top of a double boiler, combine water, lemon juice, sugar and cornstarch.
- Stir constantly over boiling water until thick and clear.
- Add a little of the hot mixture to the beaten egg yolk and whisk together well.
- Pour back into hot mixture in double boiler and cook, stirring constantly, for 1 more minute. Remove from heat and stir in lemon extract, butter and food coloring. Stir until butter dissolves.
- Cover and chill until ready to use.

Yield: 1½ cups (375 mL).

Butterhorns

- Before baking, do not make an indentation in center or put in a filling.
- Remove basic Danish from oven.
- Spread Cream Cheese Frosting, page 155, over freshly baked Danish.
- Sprinkle with finely chopped walnuts.

Bear Claws

¼ cup	butter OR margarine	60 mL
½ cup	sugar	125 mL
½ cup	finely ground almonds	125 mL

- Roll out Danish dough to a 16 x 30" (41 x 75 cm) rectangle.
- Make a paste with the butter, sugar and almonds. Spread filling over ⅔ of the length of the surface (see diagram, page 32).
- Fold dough into thirds; A over B and C over A.
- Roll dough with a rolling pin to flatten slightly. Pinch edges to seal.
- Slice ¾" (2 cm) slashes every ½" (1.3 cm) along length of sealed edge.
- Bake on a greased pan at 350°F (180°C) for 20-25 minutes.
- Remove from oven; spread with Cream Cheese Frosting, page 155, and sprinkle with sliced roasted almonds. Slice into 2" (5 cm) pieces.

Yield: 15 Bear Claws.

Bear Claws

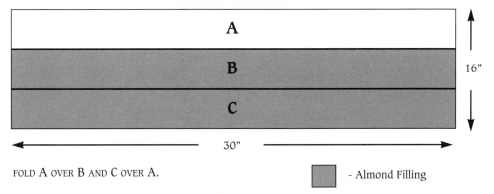

16"

30"

FOLD A OVER B AND C OVER A.

▢ - Almond Filling

Croissants

Follow recipe for Danish Pastries, page 28.

- Preheat oven to 350°F (180°C).
- Place chilled dough on counter. Roll to a 16 x 32" (41 x 82 cm) rectangle. Slice into 4 strips 4 x 32" (10 x 82 cm) each. Cut triangles (with a 4" [10 cm] bottom width on each) out of each strip. See diagram below.
- Roll from wide end up to narrow end. Place on a lightly greased 10 x 15" (25 x 38 cm) pan. Shape each roll into a "C". Brush with eggwash (1 egg beaten into 2 tbsp. [30 mL] milk). Let rise until double.
- Bake for 20 minutes, until golden brown. Serve warm with butter.

Yield: 32 croissants.

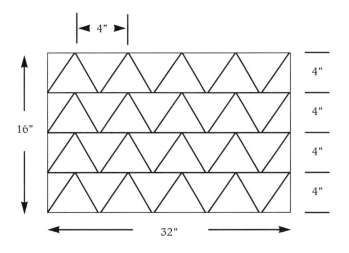

4"

16"

4"
4"
4"
4"

32"

White Bread

This excellent recipe from my friend, Debbie, also makes very good buns and cinnamon buns.

4 cups	warm water	1 L
¼ cup	honey	60 mL
2 tbsp.	yeast	30 mL
¼ cup	oil	60 mL
2 tsp.	salt	10 mL
2 tbsp.	lemon juice	30 mL
4	eggs	4
11 cups	flour (approximately)	2.75 L

- In a large mixing bowl, combine water, honey and yeast, and let sit for 10 minutes.
- Add oil, salt, lemon juice and eggs, and beat until well mixed.
- Add 5 cups (1.25 L) flour and beat well.
- Add 4 more cups (1 L) of flour, 1 cup (250 mL) at a time, until well mixed.
- Knead in remaining flour until a smooth, firm dough is formed. Knead for 10 minutes.
- Place in an oiled bowl. Turn over to ensure both sides are oiled.
- Cover and put in a warm place to rise until double in bulk, approximately 45 minutes to 1 hour.
- Punch down once.
- Form into loaves and put into 4, greased 5 x 9" (13 x 23 cm) loaf pans.
- Let rise to double in bulk, about 45 minutes.
- Bake at 350°F (180°C) for 15 minutes then reduce heat to 325°F (160°C) and bake for 30 more minutes.

Yield: 4 loaves.

Variation:

Raisin Bread: *Add 1 cup (250 mL) raisins to liquid and ½ tsp. (2 mL) cinnamon to flour.*

Buns

Light and fluffy even on the second day.

4½ cups	warm water	1.125 L
⅔ cup	sugar	150 mL
½ cup	melted shortening OR lard OR oil	125 mL
1 tbsp.	salt	15 mL
1 tbsp.	vinegar	15 mL
1 tbsp.	yeast	15 mL
10-12 cups	flour	2.5-3 L

- In a large mixing bowl, combine warm water, sugar, shortening, salt, vinegar and 2 cups (500 mL) of the flour.
- Beat until smooth.
- Sprinkle yeast over mixture. Let stand 5 minutes then beat.
- Add remaining flour, 1 cup (250 mL) at a time, until a smooth but stiff dough is formed.
- Knead for about 5 minutes, until dough is smooth and elastic but not sticky.
- Place dough in a greased covered bowl, in a warm place, until double in bulk (about 45 minutes).
- Punch dough down and let rise 15 more minutes.
- Form into rounds the size of golf balls and place in 2, 10 x 15" (25 x 38 cm) baking pans.
- Let rise until double in size, 35-40 minutes.
- Bake at 350°F (180°C) for 20 minutes.
- Remove from oven and grease tops of buns with buttered wax paper.
- Invert onto cooling racks.

Yield: 3 dozen buns.

Lord, when we are wrong make us willing to change.
And when we are right make us easy to live with.

Buns

Continued

Variations:

Sesame Seed Buns: After second rising, shape dough and brush unbaked buns with a mixture of 1 beaten egg white and 1 tbsp. (15 mL) milk. Sprinkle with sesame seeds. Let rise again as in step nine and bake as on page 34.

Whole-Wheat Buns: Add 2 tbsp. (30 mL) molasses. Use brown sugar instead of white. Substitute 4 cups (1 L) whole-wheat flour for that amount of all-purpose flour.

Hamburger Buns: After second rising, divide dough into 24 pieces. Roll into balls and flatten. You may sprinkle with sesame seeds. Follow the directions for Sesame Seed Buns.

Onion Buns: Add 1¼ oz. (37 g) pkg. dry onion soup mix or 2 tbsp. (30 mL) of dry onion flakes to wet ingredients. Do not add salt. Let dough rise twice and shape like Hamburger Buns. Brush with egg white and 1 tbsp. (15 mL) milk and sprinkle with poppy seeds. Let rise again as in step nine and bake as on previous page.

Cheese Buns: Add 1 cup (250 mL) grated cheese or small cheese cubes to dough. Let dough rise twice and prepare like Hamburger Buns. Halfway through baking, sprinkle more grated cheese on top.

Pizza Buns: Prepare like Hamburger Buns. Brush pizza sauce thinly but evenly over buns before putting them to rise for the final time. Just before baking sprinkle with grated mozzarella cheese.

Submarine Buns: After second rising, divide dough into 24 pieces. Roll each piece into a 3 x 6" (7 x 15 cm) rectangle. Roll up like a jelly roll. Seal edges. Brush with egg white mixed with 1 tbsp. (15 mL) milk. Sprinkle with sesame seeds or poppy seeds. Let rise again as in step nine and bake as on previous page.

50% Whole-Wheat Bread

Good flavor with a light texture.

4¾ cups	warm water	1.175 L
⅓ cup	sugar	75 mL
2 tbsp.	molasses	30 mL
⅓ cup	melted shortening	75 mL
2 tbsp.	yeast	30 mL
1 tbsp.	salt	15 mL
4 cups	whole-wheat flour	1 L
5-6 cups	all-purpose flour	1.25-1.5 L
½ cup	chopped sunflower seeds (optional)	125 mL

- In a large mixing bowl, combine water, sugar, molasses and shortening. Stir until sugar is dissolved.
- Sprinkle yeast over water mixture. Let stand 5 minutes. (If using Fermipan or other instant yeast continue on to next step immediately.)
- Add salt and whole-wheat flour. Beat until smooth.
- Add all-purpose flour, 1 cup (250 mL) at a time, mixing well after each addition until you have a smooth, elastic dough.
- Knead in the last cup (250 mL) of flour for about 5 minutes, until dough is no longer sticky.
- Form dough into a large ball and place in a greased bowl. Cover and place in a warm spot to rise.
- Let rise for 45 minutes, or until double. Punch down and let rise for 15 minutes more.
- Punch down again and divide dough into 4 equal portions, about 20 oz. (625 g) each.
- Shape into loaves and place into 4, greased 5 x 9"(13 x 23 cm) loaf pans.
- Let rise until double.
- Bake 15 minutes at 350°F (180°C) then 30 minutes at 300°F (150°C).

Yield: 4 loaves.

Variation:
Multi-Grain Bread: *Add ½ cup (125 mL) Sunny Boy cereal to bread dough. Brush unbaked loaf with 1 egg white mixed with 2 tbsp. (30 mL) milk and sprinkle with rolled oats.*

Basic Sourdough Starter (Monster)

Old gold rush prospectors would keep sourdough starter warm by sleeping with it beside them in bed.

2 cups	milk	500 mL
2 cups	flour	500 mL
1 tsp.	yeast	5 mL

- Combine milk, flour and yeast in a plastic or glass container. DO NOT USE A METAL CONTAINER TO STORE SOURDOUGH STARTER.
- Cover loosely or use a cheesecloth to cover.
- Keep at room temperature for 3 days. Stir down occasionally.
- After the 3-day period, store in refrigerator at least 1 day before using. Keep unused portion in refrigerator. Warm to room temperature before using in recipes.
- Sourdough causes baking to rise because it produces carbon dioxide bubbles as it works and it also produces acid.
- Baking soda is added to sourdough recipes to neutralize the acid.
- FEED YOUR STARTER EVERY WEEK WITH THE FOLLOWING INGREDIENTS, WHETHER YOU HAVE USED IT OR NOT!

1 cup	flour	250 mL
2 tbsp.	sugar	30 mL
1 cup	milk	250 mL

Three may keep a secret —
if two of them are dead.

Sourdough Pancakes

These are especially good cooked over an outdoor griddle when camping.

1 cup	flour	250 mL
2 tbsp.	sugar	30 mL
2 tsp.	baking powder	10 mL
½ tsp.	baking soda	2 mL
½ tsp.	salt	2 mL
1 cup	sourdough starter, at room temperature	250 mL
1	egg	1
½ cup	lukewarm milk OR buttermilk	125 mL
2 tbsp.	oil	30 mL

- In a medium-sized mixing bowl, combine flour, sugar, baking powder, baking soda and salt.
- Make a well in dry ingredients.
- In a small bowl, mix together starter, egg, milk and oil.
- Pour wet ingredients into the well in the dry ingredients; mix until moistened.
- Spoon and spread batter onto a hot oiled griddle.

Yield: 8 pancakes.

Note: *This batter will get thick and bubbly. DO NOT STIR DOWN!!*

Hint: *Warm sourdough starter to room temperature in your microwave on a low setting (e.g., defrost, for 2-3 minutes).*

When doubling this recipe, do not double baking soda.

Well done is better than well said.

Sourdough English Muffins

1 cup	sourdough starter, at room temperature	250 mL
1 tsp.	yeast	5 mL
¾ cup	buttermilk, lukewarm	175 mL
1 tsp.	sugar	5 mL
1 tsp.	baking soda	5 mL
2½ cups	flour	625 mL
½ tsp.	salt	2 mL
¼ cup	cornmeal, for sprinkling on top	60 mL

- Combine sourdough starter, buttermilk, baking soda, yeast and sugar in a medium-sized mixing bowl. Add 2 cups (500 mL) flour with salt. Knead in remaining flour and roll to ¾" (2 cm) thickness; cut into 3" (7 cm) circles.
- Dip muffins in cornmeal on both sides. Let stand in a warm place for 1 hour.
- Fry on a lightly greased griddle turning frequently, about 20 minutes total.
- Turn when lightly brown and brown on other side. Serve with butter and jam.

Yield: 10 English muffins.

Hint: *Use a 3" (7 cm) round cutter, wide-mouth Mason jar lid or empty tuna can for cutting circles.*

Sourdough French Bread

2 tbsp.	yeast	30 mL
1 cup	sourdough starter, at room temperature	250 mL
2½ cups	warm water	625 mL
¼ cup	sugar	60 mL
⅓ cup	shortening, melted	75 mL
2 tsp.	salt	10 mL
½ tsp.	baking soda	2 mL
6-7 cups	flour	1.5-1.75 L

- Combine yeast, sourdough starter, warm water and sugar in a large mixing bowl. Let stand 5 minutes. Add melted shortening, salt, baking soda and half the flour. Beat. Stir in as much of the remaining flour as possible. Knead in the rest of the flour until you have a smooth stiff dough.
- Let rest 15 minutes and punch down. Let rise another 15 minutes and again punch down. Do this twice more for a total of 4 punch-downs and restings.
- Divide dough into 2 pieces and roll into 2 oblong loaves.
- Place both loaves on a greased baking sheet and let rise for 30 minutes.
- Bake for 30-35 minutes in a 375°F (190°C) oven.

Yield: 2 loaves.

Herb and Garlic Bread

Serve with a barbecue or your favorite Italian pasta dish.

1	loaf French Bread (See Sourdough French Bread, page 39)	1
⅓ cup	butter	75 mL
¼ tsp.	garlic powder	1 mL
½ tsp.	dried basil leaves	2 mL
1 tbsp.	grated Parmesan cheese	15 mL

- Preheat oven to 350°F (180°C).
- In a small bowl, combine butter, garlic, basil and Parmesan cheese. Cream with a fork or spoon until well mixed.
- Slice bread in 1" (2.5 cm) slices.
- Spread with butter mixture on 1 side of each piece of bread.
- Stack pieces to form a loaf.
- Cover loosely with foil and bake for 10 minutes, or until loaf is hot and butter is melted into bread.

Yield: 1 loaf.

Sourdough Cheesebread

This recipe also makes 12 delicious muffins.

2 cups	flour	500 mL
1 tbsp.	sugar	15 mL
1 tbsp.	baking powder	15 mL
½ tsp.	baking soda	2 mL
½ tsp.	salt	2 mL
1 tbsp.	dry parsley flakes	15 mL
1 cup	grated sharp Cheddar	250 mL
½ cup	sourdough starter, at room temperature	125 mL
1 cup	warm milk	250 mL
1	egg	1
½ cup	melted shortening	125 mL

- Preheat oven to 350°F (180°C).
- In a medium-sized mixing bowl, combine flour, sugar, baking powder, baking soda, salt, parsley and cheese.

Sourdough Cheesebread

Continued

- In a small bowl, combine sourdough starter, milk, egg and melted shortening, mixing well.
- Make a well in the middle of dry ingredients. Pour wet mixture into the well.
- Stir until moistened. DO NOT OVERMIX.
- Spoon into a greased 5 x 9" (13 x 23 cm) loaf pan. Let sit for 5 minutes.
- Bake for 45 minutes. If baking muffins, bake for 20-25 minutes.

Yield: 1 loaf.

See photograph of muffins on page 69.

Sourdough Bran Muffins

½ cup	sourdough starter, at room temperature	125 mL
1 cup	warm sour milk	250 mL
1 cup	bran	250 mL
¼ cup	butter OR margarine	60 mL
½ cup	sugar	125 mL
1	egg	1
2 tbsp.	molasses	30 mL
1¼ cups	flour	300 mL
½ tsp.	salt	2 mL
½ tsp.	baking soda	2 mL
1 tsp.	baking powder	5 mL
½ cup	raisins, chopped dates OR walnuts	125 mL

- Preheat oven to 350°F (180°C).
- In a small bowl, combine sourdough starter, sour milk and bran. Set aside.
- In a medium-sized bowl, cream butter and sugar together.
- Add egg and molasses; beat until light and fluffy.
- Combine flour, salt, baking soda and baking powder.
- Add sourdough mixture to sugar mixture, alternately with dry ingredients.
- Stir in raisins.
- Pour into 12 large, greased or lined muffin cups, filling to the top.
- Bake for 20-25 minutes.

Yield: 12 large muffins.

Hint: *To make sour milk add 1 tbsp. (15 mL) of lemon juice to milk and let stand for 10-15 minutes.*

Sourdough Doughnuts

This is an adaptation of a regular doughnut recipe from my friend Emily.
These are very light and fluffy

½ cup	sourdough starter, at room temperature	125 mL
3½ cups	warm water	875 mL
6	egg yolks	6
1 tbsp.	salt	15 mL
1 cup	sugar	250 mL
½ tsp.	baking soda	2 mL
2 tbsp.	yeast	30 mL
3 cups	flour	750 mL
¾ cup	oil	175 mL
6-7 cups	flour	1.5-1.75 L

- In a large bowl, combine warmed starter, water, egg yolks, salt, sugar and baking soda. Whisk until well mixed.
- Sprinkle yeast over mixture and set aside for about 5 minutes.
- In a separate bowl, combine 3 cups (750 mL) flour and oil. Mix with fingertips or a spoon until crumbly. Add to the starter mixture and stir until smooth.
- Add enough of the remaining flour to make a soft dough. Knead until smooth and elastic. Place in a lightly oiled bowl and cover. Let rise in a warm place until double in bulk.
- Punch down and let rise again for about 15 more minutes.
- Punch down again and roll out on an oiled surface to ½" (1.3 cm) thickness.
- Cut with a floured doughnut cutter. Place uncooked doughnuts on an oiled surface and cover.
- Let rise until double, about 45 minutes.
- Fry in deep hot oil, 375°F (190°C), until light brown on the bottom; flip over and fry until the other side is light brown.
- Remove and drain on paper toweling.
- While still warm, dip in glaze or other coatings.

Yield: 3 dozen doughnuts.

Sugar Glaze: *Combine 2 cups (500 mL) sugar and ⅓ cup (75 mL) water; beat until smooth. Dip whole doughnuts in glaze.*

Chocolate Glaze: *Combine 2 cups (500 mL) icing sugar, ⅓ cup (75 mL) cocoa, ¼ cup (75 mL) water. Beat until smooth. Dip tops of doughnuts in chocolate.*

Sugar Coating: *Pour sugar into a paper bag; shake 1 doughnut at a time.*

Snacks
&
Beverages

Smoked Cheese Ball

2 x 8 oz.	cream cheese	2 x 250 g
1 tsp.	Worcestershire sauce	5 mL
½ tsp	seasoning salt	2 mL
2 tbsp.	mayonnaise	30 mL
5	drops Louisiana hot sauce OR Tabasco sauce	5
1 cup	grated Cheddar cheese	250 mL
8 oz.	hickory-smoked Gouda cheese, grated	250 g
1 tbsp.	chopped green onion OR chives	15 mL
	chopped pecans OR walnuts	

- Combine the cream cheese, Worcestershire sauce, seasoned salt, mayonnaise and hot sauce, and beat until light and fluffy.
- Beat in the grated Cheddar and hickory-smoked cheeses.
- Stir in the chives.
- Form into a large ball and roll in chopped nuts.
- Serve on a platter with assorted crackers.

Serves 20.

Variation: *For Christmas parties form into a Yule Log.*

Ham, Cheese and Pineapple Ball

2 x 8 oz.	cream cheese	2 x 250 g
¾ cup	well-drained crushed pineapple	175 mL
1 tsp.	seasoned salt	5 mL
1 cup	grated Cheddar cheese	250 mL
1 cup	finely chopped OR cubed ham	250 mL
¼ cup	chopped green pepper	60 mL
	chopped pecans OR walnuts	

- Beat the cream cheese and pineapple together until smooth.
- Stir in seasoned salt and remaining ingredients except nuts.
- Form into a ball and roll in nuts.
- Serve with crackers.

Serves 20.

Variation: *Garnish with chopped red and green cherries at Christmas.*

Minty Fruit Dip

This cool dip for hot summer days is perfect with fresh fruit. It is especially delicious with cantaloupe and honeydew melon.

1 cup	whipping cream	250 mL
4 oz.	cream cheese, softened	125 g
½ cup	icing sugar	125 mL
1-2 tbsp.	crème de menthe syrup OR to taste	15-30 mL

- Whip cream in a small bowl and set aside.
- Beat cream cheese and icing sugar together.
- Beat in crème de menthe syrup until light and fluffy.
- Fold in whipped cream.

Yield: About 2 cups (500 mL).

Variations:

Strawberry, Blueberry or Raspberry Dips: *Add ¼-½ cup (60-125 mL) of puréed berries instead of crème de menthe.*

Fruit Dips: *¼ cup (60 mL) undiluted frozen fruit juice concentrate may be substituted for créme de menthe syrup.*

Yogurt Dip: *½ cup (125 mL) plain yogurt may be used instead of cream cheese but the dip will not be as firm. Keep refrigerated until ready to serve.*

One reason why a dog is such a lovable creature is that his tail wags instead of his tongue.

45

Guacamole Dip

This excellent Mexican dip is great with nachos.

8 oz.	cream cheese	250 g
½ cup	sour cream	125 mL
2	ripe avocados, peeled and mashed	2
1 cup	hot OR mild Mexican salsa OR chunky taco sauce	250 mL
1 tsp.	lemon juice	5 mL

- In a medium-sized mixing bowl, combine cream cheese, sour cream and avocados. Beat until smooth.
- Stir in salsa. Place in a covered container. Refrigerate until ready to serve.
- Serve with vegetable dippers or nacho chips.

Yield: About 3 cups (750 mL) of dip.

Hint: *This can also be made in a blender. Add salsa then remaining ingredients, blending until smooth.*

Crab Dip

Great with raw vegetables or crackers.

6.5 oz.	can crab meat (membranes removed)	184 g
8 oz.	pkg. cream cheese	250 g
¼ cup	mayonnaise	60 mL
2 tbsp.	French dressing	30 mL
2 tbsp.	ketchup	30 mL
1 tbsp.	finely sliced green onion	15 mL
1 tbsp.	lemon juice	15 mL

- In a small mixing bowl, combine all ingredients and beat until smooth.
- Refrigerate until ready to serve.
- Serve with sliced raw carrots, celery, zucchini, cauliflower, broccoli, green peppers, cucumbers, raw turnip chunks or crackers or chips.

Yield: About 3 cups (750 mL) of dip.

Variation: *Substitute broken shrimp for the crab.*

See photograph on page 51.

Appetizer Spinach Dip

A new way to serve this delicious dip.

8 slices	bacon	8 slices
10 oz.	pkg. frozen spinach	283 g
½ cup	mayonnaise	125 mL
1 cup	sour cream	250 mL
8 oz.	cream cheese	250 g
¾ cup	grated sharp Cheddar cheese	175 mL
2 tbsp.	chopped red OR green onion	30 mL
¼ tsp.	seasoning salt	1 mL
10 oz.	can water chestnuts, drained and chopped	284 mL
4.5 oz.	can broken shrimp (optional)	128 g
2	pkgs. miniature pita bread	2

- Fry and crumble bacon. Set aside.
- Thaw spinach, drain and pat dry.
- Chop into small pieces and set aside.
- In large bowl, combine mayonnaise, sour cream and cream cheese. Beat well.
- Stir in spinach, grated cheese, onion, bacon, seasoning salt, water chestnuts and shrimp, if using.
- Cut each mini pita in half with scissors.
- To serve, place dip in a bowl in the middle of a platter. Arrange cut pita bread around bowl. Place a small spoon in the dip. Let everybody spoon dip into pita pockets and enjoy.

Yield: 4 cups (1 L) dip.

Variations: *For a lower calorie dip use 1 cup (250 mL) cottage cheese, puréed in blender, instead of cream cheese, and/or use 1 cup (250 mL) plain yogurt in place of sour cream.*

Also, serve with assorted crackers, crisp fresh vegetables or rye or whole-wheat bread cubes.

This dip can be served warm or cold. If serving warm, heat in an ovenproof, 1-quart (1 L) dish, covered, at 300°F (150°C) until heated through, about 20 minutes.

Cheesy Crab-Stuffed Mushroom Caps

24	medium to large mushrooms	24
½ cup	finely grated mild Cheddar cheese	125 mL
4 oz.	cream cheese	125 g
2 tbsp.	melted butter	30 mL
1	small garlic clove, crushed	1
5	drops Louisiana hot sauce	5
6.5 oz.	can crabmeat	185 g
1 tbsp.	diced green onion OR chives	15 mL

- Remove stems and scrape out the insides of mushroom caps.
- Place on a lightly greased baking sheet.
- Combine cheeses, butter, garlic and hot sauce, using a food processor, electric mixer or fork to mix until smooth.
- Stir in crabmeat and onion. Mix well.
- Spoon cheese-crab mixture into mushroom caps until they are all filled. 1-1½ tsp. (5-7 mL) should be enough for each.
- Place under broiler and broil until lightly browned.
- Serve warm. Allow to stand about 5 minutes before serving.

Yield: 24 appetizers.

Variation: *This crab filling is very also good spread on slices of French bread and broiled.*

Burrito Bites

A delicious and different appetizer.

cooked tortillas, see page 15
cream cheese
Cheddar cheese, grated
fresh spinach leaves
thinly sliced cucumber
thinly sliced smoked ham OR turkey
salsa

Burrito Bites

Continued

- Spread each tortilla with cream cheese, right to the edges.
- Sprinkle sparingly with grated Cheddar cheese.
- Place spinach leaves in a single row down the middle.
- Place very thinly sliced cucumber overlapping, along one side of the spinach.
- Place thinly sliced deli meat down the other side of the spinach.
- Take tortilla and roll up so that the spinach is lengthwise in the burrito.
- Press edges so that cream cheese holds edges together.
- Slice in 1" (2.5 cm) slices.
- Serve with salsa in a dish on the side.
- To eat, place a spoonful of salsa on top of each slice.

Potato Skins

6	medium baked potatoes	6
1/3 cup	melted butter	75 mL
1 cup	grated Cheddar, Swiss OR mozzarella cheese	250 mL
8	slices bacon, fried crisp and crumbled	8
1/3 cup	chopped green onion OR chives	75 mL
	sour cream	

- Cut each potato into 4 sections lengthwise.
- Scoop out inside of each piece leaving 1/4" (1 cm) of pulp inside each potato. Reserve pulp for another use.
- Brush sections inside and out with butter. Place on an ungreased baking sheet.
- Bake at 375°F (190°C) for 10 minutes.
- Remove from oven and sprinkle each piece with cheese, bacon and chives.
- Return to oven for a couple of minutes until cheese melts and bubbles.
- Serve with sour cream.

Yield: 24 skins.

Nachos

This is a quick and easy snack to make. Kids love them.

1	pkg. tortilla chips (any size) grated Cheddar cheese OR mozzarella diced tomatoes bacon fried crisp and crumbled fresh OR canned jalapeño peppers, sliced and seeds removed black olives, sliced green onion, sliced salsa	1

- Preheat broiler.
- Line a 10-15" (25 x 38 cm) pan or large pizza pan with tortilla chips.
- Sprinkle liberally with grated cheese.
- Sprinkle remaining ingredients on top of cheese.
- Place under a broiler and broil until cheese melts and bubbles.
- Remove from oven and serve warm with salsa and sour cream for dipping.

Yield: 1 large pan.

Variation: *If jalapeño peppers are too hot for you, try green peppers.*

It's too bad human beings can't exchange problems.
Everyone knows exactly how to solve the other person's problems.

Appetizers

Beef On-A-Stick, page 54
Rumaki, page 53
Crab Dip, page 46

Rumaki

Tasty Hawaiian bacon roll-ups. These will be the first to be eaten at any party.

1 lb.	lean bacon (about 20 slices)	500 g
10	water chestnuts	10
5	large scallops	5
	toothpicks	
¼ cup	water	60 mL
⅓ cup	soy sauce	75 mL
3 tbsp.	brown sugar OR honey	45 mL
1	small garlic clove, crushed	1
⅛ tsp.	ground ginger	0.5 mL

- Cut bacon in half, across, and cook until half-done.
- Drain well.
- Cut water chestnuts in half.
- Cut scallops into 4 pieces.
- Wrap bacon around either a water chestnut half or a piece of scallop. Fasten with a toothpick.
- Combine the water, soy sauce, brown sugar, garlic and ground ginger to make a marinade.
- Place the bacon rolls in the marinade for at least 30 minutes.
- Drain. Preheat broiler. Broil, turning once, until bacon is crispy.
- Serve hot.

Yield: 40 appetizers.

Variation: *Lightly sautéed chicken livers may also be cut in quarters, wrapped with bacon and marinated and cooked as above.*

See photograph on page 51.

Beef-On-A-Stick

1½-2 lbs.	sirloin steak OR flank steak	750 g-1 kg
¼ cup	water	60 mL
¾ cup	soy sauce	175 mL
½ cup	honey OR brown sugar	125 mL
¼ cup	oil	60 mL
1	lemon, juice of (3 tbsp. [45 mL])	1
1 tsp.	ginger	5 mL
¼ tsp.	pepper	1 mL
1	garlic clove, minced OR ⅛ tsp. (0.5 mL) garlic powder	1
	wooden skewers	

- Slice steak in thin strips (see Hint, below) and place in a bowl.
- Combine remaining ingredients to make a marinade.
- Pour marinade over beef strips and refrigerate about 3 hours or overnight.
- Preheat broiler. Soak wooden skewers in water while the meat is marinating.
- Thread meat onto skewers and place on a 10 x 15" (25 x 38 cm) pan or a broiler pan.
- Broil until meat is cooked to desired doneness.
- Brush with marinade while broiling.
- Serve hot.

Yield: About 16-24 appetizers.

Variation: *Try thinly sliced pork or chicken breasts instead of beef.*

Hint: *Slice meat when partially frozen. It's easier to slice more thinly this way. Slice across the grain.*

See photograph on page 51.

Strawberry Rhubarb Sparkling Punch

This is a delicious Spring punch. It's great for wedding receptions.

12 cups	chopped rhubarb, fresh OR frozen	3 L
12 cups	hot water	3 L
1/4 tsp.	cream of tartar	1 mL
1 1/2 cups	sugar	375 mL
1/5 oz.	pkg. strawberry Kool-Aid (unsweetened)	6 g
3/4 cup	sugar	175 mL
2 qts.	water	2 L
15 oz.	pkg. frozen sliced strawberries	425 mL
2 qts.	ginger ale, 7-Up OR sparkling mineral water	2 L

- In a large stainless steel or enamel pot or Dutch oven, combine rhubarb, hot water, cream of tartar and 1 1/2 cups (375 mL) sugar.
- Bring to a boil and simmer for 1 minute.
- Remove from heat and let stand 1 hour.
- Strain juice through a sieve into a large bowl and discard rhubarb pulp. COOL.
- Add remaining ingredients and stir to mix.

Yield: 50, 4 oz. (125 mL) servings.

Serves-A-Bunch Punch

This is terrific for family reunions or any large gathering.

12 oz.	can frozen lemonade	341 mL
12 oz.	can frozen fruit punch	341 mL
2 x 12 oz.	cans frozen orange juice	2 x 341 mL
4 qts.	ice water	4 L
2 x 2 qts.	bottles 7-Up, ginger ale OR sparkling mineral water	2 x 2 L

- In a large bowl or bucket, combine all ingredients and mix well. Transfer to a punch bowl. Add ice cubes and serve chilled.

Yield: 2 1/2 gallons (10 L).

Hint: *Add 7-Up to the punch bowl at the last minute, to ensure the punch doesn't go flat before serving.*

Banana Slush

A cool summer refresher.

12 oz.	can frozen orange juice concentrate	355 mL
12 oz.	can frozen lemonade concentrate	355 mL
4 cups	pineapple juice	1 L
5	bananas, puréed	5
4 cups	water	1 L
1 cup	sugar	250 mL
	7-Up OR ginger ale	

- In a 1-gallon (4 L) plastic container, combine all ingredients except ginger ale. Stir to mix. Freeze.
- When ready to serve, place 1 scoop of frozen slush into a glass and top with 7-Up or ginger ale. Stir well.

Yield: 3 quarts (3 L) of slush.

Variation: *Pour slush mixture into an angel food cake pan or a bundt pan and freeze. Place in a punch bowl and pour 7-Up or ginger ale over top. Stir before serving.*

Hot Christmas Wassail

This warms you up after skating or skiing, or on a cold winter's night.

1 tsp.	whole cloves	5 mL
1 tsp.	allspice berries	5 mL
2	cinnamon sticks, 6" (15 cm), broken	2
2 cups	water	500 mL
½ cup	sugar	125 mL
4 cups	apple juice	1 L
4 cups	cranberry juice	1 L
¼ tsp.	salt	1 mL

- Put spices in a cheesecloth bag.
- In a large kettle or Dutch oven, combine water and sugar and bring to a boil.
- Add the spices in the bag. Boil for 10 minutes.
- Add apple juice and cranberry juice and boil for 10 minutes more.
- Remove spices and add salt. Serve hot.

Serves 12.

Variations: *Use cranberry-raspberry juice instead of cranberry juice.*

Hot Mulled Cider: *Omit cranberry juice and add 4 additional cups (1 L) of apple juice. Add brown sugar instead of white sugar.*

Hint: *Pour Wassail into a crockpot to keep hot.*

Soups
&
Chowders

Chicken Soup Stock

3 lbs.	chicken	1.5 kg
3 qts.	water	3 L
½ tsp.	whole allspice	2 mL
½ tsp.	peppercorns	2 mL
1½ tsp.	salt	7 mL
1	bay leaf	1
1	onion, coarsely chopped	1
2	celery stalks, chopped	2
2	carrots, peeled and chopped	2

- Put everything into a large pot or a Dutch oven. Bring to a boil.
- Simmer over low heat for 1½-2 hours.
- Strain broth through a sieve into a bowl or pail. Discard vegetables and save chicken for use in soup.
- Refrigerate broth until fat floats to top and hardens.
- Skim off fat and use broth for soup or any recipe that calls for chicken stock or broth.
- This will keep for 3 days in the refrigerator. It can also be frozen.

Yield: About 3-quarts (3 L) of stock.

Chicken Gumbo Soup

11 cups	chicken broth, see above	2.75 L
28 oz.	can tomatoes, diced	796 mL
2	celery stalks, diced (1 cup [250 mL])	2
1	small onion, peeled and diced	1
2	carrots, peeled and diced	2
3	okra, thinly sliced	3
⅓ cup	rice (parboiled is best)	75 mL
2 cups	chopped cooked chicken	500 mL

- In a large soup pot or Dutch oven, combine chicken stock and tomatoes. Bring to a boil. While simmering add celery, onions, carrots and okra.
- After 10 minutes add rice and chicken. Simmer for 20-25 minutes, or until rice is cooked.

Yield: 12 cups (3 L) of soup.

Hint: *When making chicken soups, add chicken about 20 minutes prior to eating, otherwise it becomes stringy and falls apart. Likewise, add rice about 20 minutes before serving or it will split and ruin the appearance of the soup.*

Chicken-Corn Chowder

2 tbsp.	butter OR margarine	30 mL
½ cup	minced onion	125 mL
1	celery stalk, sliced	1
3 cups	chicken broth	750 mL
14 oz.	can creamed corn	398 mL
1½ cups	milk	375 mL
2	medium potatoes, peeled and diced	2
1 cup	diced chicken	250 mL
¼ tsp.	pepper	1 mL
¼ tsp.	paprika	1 mL
¼ tsp.	salt	1 mL
1 tsp.	dry parsley	5 mL
½ cup	grated mozzarella cheese	125 mL

- In a large saucepan, melt butter. Add onion and celery; sauté until transparent.
- Add chicken broth, corn and milk. Stir until well-blended.
- Add potatoes, chicken, pepper, paprika, salt and parsley.
- Simmer over medium-low heat until potatoes are cooked, about 20 minutes.
- Stir in cheese.

Serves 6.

*Nature gave man two ends — one to sit on and one to think with.
A man's success or failure depends on the one he uses the most.*

Traditional Corn Chowder

3 cups	chicken broth	750 mL
1	small onion, minced	1
2	small potatoes, diced	2
¼	medium green pepper, chopped	¼
¼ cup	celery, chopped	60 mL
3 tbsp.	minced celery leaves	45 mL
1 cup	cooked whole-kernel corn	250 mL
3	bacon slices, cooked crisp and crumbled	3
1½ cups	whole milk	375 mL
	salt and pepper to taste	
¼ tsp.	paprika	1 mL
2½ tbsp.	flour	37 mL
¼ cup	cold water	60 mL

- Heat chicken broth and add all vegetables except corn. Simmer for 15 minutes.
- Add corn, bacon, milk and seasonings.
- Combine flour with water and add to soup.
- Cook and stir until thickened.

Serves 6-8.

Chunky Split Pea Soup

2 cups	dry split peas	500 mL
1 lb.	ham, cubed	500 g
½ cup	chopped onions	125 mL
2-3	celery stalks, sliced	2-3
3	medium carrots, sliced	3
2	medium potatoes, cubed	2
2 tsp.	salt	10 mL
⅛ tsp.	pepper	0.5 mL
1	bay leaf	1
4 cups	water OR 2 cups (500 mL) ham stock and 2 cups (500 mL) water	1 L

- In a large soup pot, combine peas and ham, with water to cover. Bring to a boil, reduce heat and simmer, covered, about 45 minutes, or until peas are tender. Stir occasionally.

Chunky Split Pea Soup

Continued

- Add rest of ingredients and continue cooking until all vegetables are done, about 20 minutes.
- Remove 1 cup (250 mL) of peas and mash or purée.
- Return to soup pot and stir until soup is thick.
- Serve this hearty soup with homemade biscuits, buns or bread.

Serves 6-8.

Note: *If using ham stock, reduce salt. Taste before adding salt.*

Variation: *For Chunky Lentil Soup, substitute lentils for split peas. Add a drop or two of hot pepper sauce.*

Bean with Bacon Soup

This soup has such a good homemade flavor that you will want to go back for a second helping. The variation is equally good.

2 cups	dried navy beans	500 mL
6	slices bacon	6
6 cups	water	1.5 L
1 cup	chopped onion	250 mL
2/3 cup	diced carrots	150 mL
1/3 cup	chopped celery (leaves and all)	75 mL
2 tsp.	salt	10 mL
1	bay leaf	1
1 cup	tomato juice	250 mL

- Soak beans overnight in water to cover, then discard water and rinse.
- Fry bacon until crisp; drain on paper toweling. Crumble bacon and add to beans with the 6 cups (1.5 L) of fresh water.
- Sauté onions, carrots and celery in bacon drippings. Add to beans with seasonings and juice. Simmer until beans are cooked, about 2 hours.
- Remove 1 cup (250 mL) of beans and set aside to cool slightly.
- Place cooled 1 cup (250 mL) beans in a blender and purée to make a paste.
- Return purée to soup in pot. Stir until thickened.

Serves 8.

Variation: *For Bean with Ham Soup, substitute 1 cup (250 mL) chopped ham for bacon.*

Old-Fashioned Tomato Macaroni Soup

A good hearty soup.

8 cups	chicken broth	2 L
10 oz.	can tomato soup	284 mL
28 oz.	can tomatoes, diced	796 mL
1 tsp.	basil	5 mL
1/4 tsp.	thyme	1 mL
1/8 tsp.	ground pepper	0.5 mL
1/8 tsp.	ground cloves	0.5 mL
1 tsp.	sugar	5 mL
1	small garlic clove, crushed	1
1	large onion, chopped	1
2	celery stalks, diced (3/4 cup [175 mL])	2
2	large carrots, diced	2
1 cup	baby seashell OR elbow macaroni	250 mL
1 cup	chopped chicken (optional)	250 mL
	grated Parmesan cheese	

- In a large stock pot or Dutch oven, combine all ingredients except macaroni, chicken, if using, and Parmesan cheese.
- Bring to a boil and simmer until vegetables are almost cooked.
- Add macaroni and simmer until it is cooked, about 15 minutes.
- Serve with grated Parmesan cheese sprinkled on top.

Yield: 12 cups (3 L).

Variation: *2 cups (500 mL) of tomato sauce may be substituted for tomato soup.*

See photograph on the front cover.

62

Minestrone Soup

Who doesn't love a hot bowl of soup on a frosty day?
This one really hits the spot.

½ lb.	bulk pork sausage OR ground pork (see Homemade Sausage Meat, page 6)	250 g
1	medium onion, chopped	1
4 cups	chicken broth	1 L
4 cups	beef broth	1 L
14 oz.	can kidney beans, drained, OR 1 cup (250 mL) presoaked navy beans	398 mL
1 tsp.	Italian seasoning (or see below)	5 mL
1	garlic clove, crushed	1
1	bay leaf	1
2 tbsp.	parsley flakes	30 mL
¼ tsp.	black pepper	1 mL
½ tsp.	salt OR to taste	2 mL
1 cup	shredded zucchini	250 mL
1 cup	diced carrots	250 mL
3	celery stalks, chopped	3
1 cup	frozen OR fresh peas	250 mL
19 oz.	can tomatoes, diced	540 mL
1 cup	cut green beans	250 mL
2 cups	coarsely chopped cabbage, spinach OR other greens	500 mL
1½ cups	uncooked, small pasta (macaroni, baby seashells, broken spaghetti, etc.)	375 mL
	Parmesan cheese	

- Brown sausage or make miniature meatballs with seasoned ground pork.
- Drain off fat and reserve 2 tbsp. (30 mL).
- Fry onion in sausage fat in a large soup pot.
- Add remaining ingredients, except cabbage, pasta and Parmesan cheese.
- Bring to a boil and simmer for 20 minutes.
- Add cabbage and pasta; simmer for another 15 minutes, until noodles are cooked.
- To serve, sprinkle with grated Parmesan cheese and serve with crusty rolls or French bread.

Serves 8-10.

Hints: *To make Italian seasoning, combine 1 tsp. (5 mL) basil, 1 tsp. (5 mL) oregano and ½ tsp. (2 mL) thyme.*

Freeze shredded zucchini in the summer for soups during winter months.

Beefy Vegetable Soup

This is a good hearty soup that everyone will love. It is very economical to make.

1 lb.	ground beef OR chopped cooked beef	500 g
½ cup	chopped onion	125 mL
1 cup	sliced celery	250 mL
2	medium carrots, diced	2
28 oz.	can tomatoes, chopped	796 mL
1 tsp.	salt	1 mL
¼ tsp.	pepper	1 mL
4 cups	water	1 L
4 cups	beef broth	1 L
1 tsp.	Worcestershire sauce	5 mL
7.5 oz.	can tomato sauce	213 mL
¼ tsp.	dried thyme	1 mL
¼ tsp.	dried basil	1 mL
1 tsp.	sugar	5 mL
2 cups	cubed potatoes	500 mL
½ cup	barley	125 mL
1 cup	frozen OR fresh peas	250 mL

- In a large heavy soup pot or Dutch oven, brown ground beef and onion. Drain off fat. If using leftover cooked beef omit the browning step and add it to the liquid with the onion.
- Add remaining ingredients, except peas, and bring to a boil over medium heat.
- Reduce heat to medium-low and simmer, covered, for 30 minutes, or until barley and vegetables are tender.
- Add peas and simmer for 10 minutes.
- Serve with buns or biscuits.

Yield: 16 cups (4 L).

Note: *The longer this simmers the better it tastes. This can be made in a slow cooker in the morning and simmer all day for a hearty supper.*

Creamy Potato Soup

This is a meal in itself.

10	medium potatoes, peeled and chopped	10
2	medium carrots, chopped	2
2	celery stalks, chopped	2
½ cup	chopped onion	125 mL
1	small garlic clove, crushed	1
1 tsp.	salt	5 mL
¼ tsp.	pepper	1 mL
3 cups	chicken broth	750 mL
	water	
¾ cup	butter OR margarine	175 mL
1½ tsp.	salt	7 mL
¾ cup	flour	175 mL
4 cups	milk	1 L
	parsley	
	crisp crumbled bacon OR grated Cheddar cheese for garnish	

- In a large soup pot or Dutch oven, combine potatoes, carrots, celery, onion, garlic, salt and pepper.
- Add chicken broth and enough water to cover vegetables.
- Bring to a boil and simmer until vegetables are cooked, about 15 minutes. Do not drain.
- In another medium-sized pot, melt butter and stir in salt and flour to make a smooth paste.
- Whisk in milk to make a smooth sauce.
- Stir sauce into soup. Cook until thickened. This is quite a thick soup. Thin with milk if you prefer it thinner. Stir in small amounts at a time until it reaches the desired consistency.
- Serve with crumbled bacon or grated Cheddar cheese as a garnish.

Serves 12.

Variation: *Cut potatoes into small and larger cubes for an interesting texture.*

Clam Chowder: *Add 5 oz. (142 g) can baby clams with juice for the last 5 minutes of cooking.*

Basic Low-Cal Cream Soup

Substitute the sauce variation of this recipe for condensed canned cream soups.

6 cups	cold milk, skim, 1% OR 2%	1.5 L
½ tsp.	salt	2 mL
¼ cup	cornstarch	60 mL
4 tsp.	instant chicken bouillon granules	20 mL

- In a large pot or large double boiler, combine milk, salt and cornstarch.
- Cook over medium-low heat, stirring constantly until hot. Do not boil.
- Stir in chicken bouillon granules and salt.
- Stir soup over medium-low heat until it thickens and the cornstarch is cooked.
- FOR A THICK SAUCE REDUCE MILK TO 4 CUPS (1 L).

Serves 8.

Variations: *Try the following variations or make up your own, e.g., Cream of Celery, Cream of Corn, Cream of Chicken, etc.*

Low-Cal Cream of Vegetable Soup

To Basic Low-Cal Cream Soup, add to cold milk mixture:

1	celery stalk, finely sliced	1
1½ cups	frozen mixed vegetables	375 mL
2 tbsp.	chopped onion	30 mL

- Cook over medium heat until vegetables are tender or parboil vegetables before adding to soup.

Low-Cal Cream of Mushroom Soup

To Basic Low-Cal Cream Soup, add:

2 tsp.	each beef granules and chicken granules	10 mL
5⅔ cups	milk, instead of 6 cups (1.5 L)	1.4 L
¼ cup	finely chopped onion	60 mL
10 oz.	can mushroom stems and pieces OR	(284 mL)
	¼ lb. (115 g) fresh mushrooms, sliced	
⅓ cup	mushroom liquid OR leave milk at	75 mL
	6 cups (1.5 L)	

- FOR A THICK MUSHROOM SAUCE, USE ONLY 4 CUPS (1 L) OF MILK. 1 cup (250 mL) of sauce may be substituted for 1 can [10 oz. (284 mL)] of condensed cream of mushroom soup.

Low-Cal Cream of Potato Soup

To Basic Low-Cal Cream Soup, add:

²/₃ cup	chopped, parboiled onion	150 mL
2	celery stalks, thinly sliced, parboiled	2
1	large carrot, thinly sliced OR chopped, parboiled	1
2	large potatoes, chopped, parboiled	2
4	strips of bacon, cooked and crumbled for garnish grated cheese	4

Variation: *For Low-Cal Cheesy Potato Soup, add ¹/₂ cup (125 mL) grated low-fat Cheddar cheese.*

Low-Cal Vegetable Cheese Soup

To Basic Low-Cal Cream Soup, add:

1 cup	grated low-fat Cheddar cheese	250 mL
2	carrots, sliced and parboiled	2
1 cup	cauliflower florets, parboiled	250 mL
1 cup	broccoli florets, parboiled	250 mL
1	celery stalk, diced, parboiled	1

Low-Cal Clam Chowder

To Basic Low-Cal Cream of Potato Soup, add:

14 oz.	can clams (reserve juice)	398 mL
¹/₂ cup	clam juice to replace ¹/₂ cup (125 mL) of milk	125 mL

Pumpkin Chowder

This may sound unusual, but try it — you'll like it.

4 cups	peeled, cubed potatoes	1 L
1 cup	sliced carrots	250 mL
½ cup	chopped celery	125 mL
½ cup	finely chopped onion	125 mL
2 tbsp.	finely chopped green pepper	30 mL
2 cups	chicken broth	500 mL
¼ cup	butter OR margarine	60 mL
⅓ cup	water	75 mL
3 tbsp.	flour	45 mL
1½ cups	pumpkin purée OR 14 oz. (398 mL) can	375 mL
1½ tsp.	salt	7 mL
⅛ tsp.	pepper	0.5 mL
1-2 tsp.	parsley flakes	5-10 mL
1 tsp.	sugar	5 mL
2 cups	water	500 mL
1 cup	milk	250 mL
	grated Cheddar cheese	

- In a heavy soup pot, combine potatoes, carrots, celery, onion, green pepper, and the chicken broth.
- Cook at medium boil for 10 minutes. Add butter.
- Mix the ⅓ cup (75 mL) water and flour with a fork, until smooth, and pour into the soup pot.
- Add pumpkin, salt, pepper, parsley, sugar and 2 cups (500 mL) of water. Reduce heat and cook on low until vegetables are tender, about 30 minutes.
- Stir in milk and heat until hot.
- Serve bowls of soup with a garnish of grated cheese.

Serves 8.

Salad

The Ultimate Spinach Salad, page 73
Sourdough Cheesebread Muffins, page 40

Salads
&
Vegetables

Oriental Chicken Salad

A delightful addition to a summer buffet.

4 cups	shredded Chinese cabbage	1 L
1/3 cup	chopped green onion OR chives	75 mL
3/4 cup	sliced fresh mushrooms	175 mL
3/4 cup	chopped celery	175 mL
1 cup	fresh bean sprouts	250 mL
1	large carrot, peeled and cut in julienne strips	1
1 cup	small broccoli florets	250 mL
1/2 cup	thinly sliced water chestnuts	125 mL
1/2 cup	blanched sliced almonds, roasted	125 mL
1/3 cup	roasted shelled sunflower seeds	75 mL
2 cups	chopped cooked chicken breast	500 mL
	chow mein noodles (dry type)	

Soy Honey Dressing:

1/4 cup	soy sauce	60 mL
2 tbsp.	vinegar	30 mL
1/4 cup	water	60 mL
1 tbsp.	oil	15 mL
3 tbsp.	honey	45 mL

- In a large bowl, mix together the first 10 ingredients. Set aside.
- In a small bowl combine the dressing ingredients.
- Add cooked chicken to dressing and marinate for 30 minutes.
- Pour chicken and dressing over the vegetable mixture and toss until vegetables are well coated.
- Serve immediately with chow mein noodles sprinkled on top.

Serves 12.

Hint: *Simmer chicken breast in water until juices run clear, about 20 minutes. Cool and slice or chop as needed.*

The Ultimate Spinach Salad

This beautiful, nutritious main-course fruit and meat salad on a bed of spinach, has many possible variations.

1	bunch fresh spinach, washed and torn, stems removed	1
2 cups	thinly sliced, cooked chicken, turkey, pork OR beef	500 mL
2	oranges, peeled and chopped in bite-sized pieces	2
1 cup	strawberries, halved OR quartered	250 mL
1 cup	seedless red OR green grapes, halved	250 mL
2	celery stalks, sliced	2
	sunflower seeds OR cashews (optional)	

Orange Yogurt Dressing:

1 cup	plain yogurt	250 mL
1/3 cup	unsweetened frozen orange juice concentrate, undiluted	75 mL
3 tbsp.	honey, warmed until runny	45 mL
1 tsp.	poppy seeds	5 mL

- Prepare spinach and set aside.
- In a large bowl, combine meat, fruits and celery. Toss to mix; set aside.
- In a small bowl, combine yogurt, orange juice and honey. Stir until blended and smooth. Stir in poppy seeds.
- Pour over fruit and meat mixture. Stir gently to coat thoroughly.
- To serve, evenly distribute spinach leaves on plates. Spoon fruit and meat mixture onto spinach. Sprinkle with sunflower seeds or cashews.
- Serve with fresh buns.

Yield: 4 large OR 6 medium servings.

Variations: *Try thinly sliced barbecued chicken or beef in this salad for a flavorful variation.*

1 can of mandarin oranges, drained, can be used instead of fresh oranges.

See photograph on page 69.

Deluxe Spinach Salad

This salad was introduced to me by my sister, Cheryl, in Calgary.
Even spinach haters will love this salad.

2	bunches fresh crisp spinach, OR 10 oz. (285 g) bag	2
1	small head iceberg lettuce	1
½	purple onion, thinly sliced into rings	½
¾ lb.	fresh mushrooms, sliced	340 g
¾ lb.	Swiss cheese, grated	340 g
½ lb.	bacon, fried crisp and crumbled	250 g
1 cup	cottage cheese, drained, rinsed with cold water and drained again OR dry curd cottage cheese	250 mL

Mustard Poppy Seed Dressing:

½ tsp.	salt	2 mL
⅓ cup	vinegar	75 mL
⅓ cup	sugar	75 mL
½ tsp.	prepared mustard	2 mL
¾ cup	oil	175 mL
1 tsp.	poppy seeds	5 mL

- Tear cleaned spinach and lettuce into bite-sized pieces.
- In a large bowl, combine spinach, lettuce, onion rings and mushrooms.
- Just before serving, add Swiss cheese, crumbled bacon and drained cottage cheese. Toss thoroughly.
- Combine salt, vinegar, sugar and mustard in a blender or food processor.
- While blender is running, slowly drizzle the oil into the vinegar mixture.
- Stir in poppy seeds with a spoon.
- Quickly pour dressing over salad, toss and serve immediately as this does go soggy if it sits too long before serving.

Serves 12.

Variations: *Substitute lemon juice for vinegar in dressing. Substitute chopped green onion for purple onion.*

Hint: *If you are taking this salad to a potluck dinner, combine spinach, lettuce and onion in a large bowl. Put remaining ingredients into separate containers or plastic bags; bring along dressing in a container. Assemble just before serving. Shake dressing and toss with salad.*

See photograph on page 87.

74

Caesar Salad

This salad goes well with most Italian main courses.

2	heads Romaine lettuce, washed and torn	2
1 tbsp.	Parmesan cheese	15 mL
8	slices bacon, fried crisp and crumbled	8
1½ cups	croûtons	375 mL
¼ cup	freshly grated Parmesan cheese	60 mL

Dressing:

1	garlic clove, crushed	1
½ tsp.	salt	2 mL
1 tbsp.	anchovy paste (optional but good)	15 mL
3	eggs	3
1⅔ cups	oil	400 mL
3 tbsp.	lemon juice	45 mL
2 tbsp.	vinegar	30 mL
2 tbsp.	grated Parmesan cheese	30 mL
¼ tsp.	pepper	1 mL

- To prepare salad, toss first 3 ingredients together.
- To prepare the dressing, in a blender, combine garlic, salt, anchovy paste and 1 egg. Blend until puréed.
- Add 2 more eggs and blend again until everything is well mixed.
- In a measuring cup, combine oil, lemon juice and vinegar.
- Turn on blender and add oil mixture in a slow stream.
- Blend until the consistency is like mayonnaise.
- Stir in Parmesan cheese and pepper.
- Just before serving add dressing to salad and toss.
- Add croûtons and remaining ¼ cup (60 mL) Parmesan cheese and toss again lightly.

Serves 12.

Note: *If you prefer a thinner dressing add a little bit of milk and stir until you get the consistency you like. This dressing will keep for up to 1 week in the refrigerator.*

Zesty Ranch-Style Dressing

This is a creamy flavorful homemade salad dressing.
Try it the next time you have a tossed green salad.

2 cups	mayonnaise OR salad dressing	500 mL
1 cup	sour cream	250 mL
1 cup	buttermilk	250 mL
2 tbsp.	grated Parmesan cheese	30 mL
1 tbsp.	chopped fresh chives, OR 1 tsp. (5 mL) dry onion flakes OR 1 tsp. (5 mL) dry chives	15 mL
1/4 tsp.	dry mustard	1 mL
1	small garlic clove, crushed	1
1/4 tsp.	pepper	1 mL
1/2 tsp.	seasoned salt	2 mL
1/4 tsp.	dry tarragon flakes	1 mL
1 tsp.	dry parsley flakes	5 mL
1/4 tsp.	onion powder	1 mL

- Combine all ingredients in a blender. Blend until smooth. Chill and serve with green salads or as a dip for vegetables.
- Store in refrigerator and use within 2 weeks.

Yield: 4 cups (1 L).

Calico Bean Salad

This very colorful salad will brighten up any buffet table.

14 oz.	can green beans, drained	398 mL
14 oz.	can yellow beans, drained	398 mL
14 oz.	can kidney beans, drained	398 mL
14 oz.	can garbanzo beans, (chick-peas), drained	398 mL
14 oz.	can lima beans, drained	398 mL
1	large green pepper, finely chopped	1
1	red pepper, finely chopped	1
1	large onion (red OR white), sliced in thin rings	1
1/2 cup	oil	125 mL
1/2 cup	sugar	125 mL
1/2 cup	vinegar	125 mL

Calico Bean Salad

Continued

- Pour all beans into a colander and rinse with cold water.
- When drained, pour into a large bowl.
- Add green pepper, red pepper and onion.
- Mix oil, sugar and vinegar together in a blender or beat with a whisk until sugar is dissolved.
- Pour over salad and stir to evenly coat the beans.
- Chill overnight or at least 8 hours. Stir occasionally.

Serves about 12.

Cottage Cheese Salad Mold

2 x 3 oz.	pkgs. lime gelatin	2 x 85 g
2 cups	boiling water	500 mL
1 cup	cold water	250 mL
2 tsp.	mild horseradish	10 mL
¼ cup	mayonnaise OR salad dressing	60 mL
2 cups	cottage cheese	500 mL
14 oz.	can crushed pineapple, drained	398 mL

- In a large bowl, dissolve gelatin in boiling water. Stir in cold water.
- Refrigerate until partially set then beat with mixer.
- Beat in horseradish and mayonnaise.
- Stir in cottage cheese and crushed pineapple.
- Pour into a jelly mold or bowl.
- Refrigerate until firm.
- Serve on lettuce leaves.

Serves 8.

Cranberry Raspberry Fruit Mold

This is excellent with turkey or chicken dinners.

2 x 3 oz.	pkgs. raspberry gelatin	2 x 85 g
2 cups	boiling water	500 mL
4 cups	ice cubes	1 L
⅔ cup	whole berry cranberry sauce	150 mL
14 oz.	can crushed pineapple, drained	398 mL
2 tbsp.	mayonnaise OR salad dressing	30 mL
1 cup	whipping cream, whipped	250 mL

- In a large bowl, mix gelatin and boiling water until dissolved.
- Stir in ice cubes until gelatin is partially set. Discard any unthawed ice cubes.
- Remove 1 cup (250 mL) gelatin and set aside.
- Add cranberry sauce and drained crushed pineapple to gelatin in large bowl.
- Pour into an 8" (20 cm) square baking dish or an 8" (20 cm) round dish. Place in refrigerator.
- In a small bowl, beat together 1 cup (250 mL) gelatin and mayonnaise until smooth.
- Fold in whipped cream.
- Spread over set gelatin mixture in pan.
- Refrigerate for at least 2 hours, or until firm.

Serves 12-14.

Variation: *1 cup (250 mL) of fresh raspberries or a 14 oz. (398 mL) can drained fruit cocktail may be substituted for crushed pineapple.*

No difficulties, no discovery; no pains, no gains.

Stuffed Baked Potatoes

These can be served as a side dish with any meat or fish or they can be the entrée served with buns and a salad.

6	large baking potatoes	6
⅓ cup	melted butter	75 mL
½ cup	milk, OR ¼ cup (60 mL) each milk and sour cream	125 mL
½ tsp.	salt	2 mL
2 tbsp.	butter	30 mL
¼ tsp.	pepper	1 mL
⅛ tsp.	onion powder	0.5 mL
1 cup	grated Cheddar cheese	250 mL
1 tbsp.	finely chopped fresh chives	15 mL

- Wash and scrub potatoes. Slit a cross on the top of each potato. Wrap in foil; bake 1 hour at 400°F (200°C), or until potatoes are cooked. Leave oven on.
- Remove potatoes from oven and cut a thick slice from the side of the potato that has the cross on it.
- Scrape the pulp from the slices, put in a medium-sized bowl and discard the skins.
- Scoop out the rest of the potatoes leaving at least a ¼" (1 cm) shell. Leave shell whole.
- Add the potato pulp to the pulp in the bowl.
- Brush shells with melted butter and return to oven for 5 minutes, or until slightly crispy; set aside.
- Add all remaining ingredients, except cheese and chives, to potato pulp and mash or beat until smooth.
- Stir in cheese and chives and spoon into potato shells.
- Bake 15 minutes at 400°F (200°C), until lightly browned.

Serves 6.

Variations:

Crab:	*Add 6.5 oz. (184 g) can flaked crab and substitute Swiss cheese for Cheddar.*
Ham:	*Add 1 cup (250 mL) cubed ham.*
Hamburger:	*Add ½ lb. (250 g) fried and drained lean ground beef.*
Mushroom:	*Add ½ cup (125 mL) chopped mushrooms, sautéed.*

Creamy Potato Casserole

This recipe comes from my friend Annalee from Utah. When she was growing up her mother served these potatoes with ham or chicken.

7	medium potatoes	7
½ cup	butter OR margarine, melted	125 mL
1 cup	mushroom sauce, page 66, OR 10 oz. (284 mL) can of mushroom soup	250 mL
2 cups	sour cream	500 mL
1 cup	grated Cheddar cheese	250 mL
¼ cup	chopped green onion	60 mL
1 cup	crushed cornflakes	250 mL
2 tbsp.	melted butter	30 mL

- Boil potatoes until tender but firm. Drain.
- Preheat oven to 350°F (180°).
- Grate potatoes into a greased 9 x 13" (23 x 33 cm) pan. Distribute evenly.
- In a bowl, combine melted butter, mushroom sauce and sour cream. Whisk together well.
- Stir in cheese and chopped green onion.
- Pour creamy mixture evenly over grated potatoes. DO NOT STIR TOGETHER.
- Take 2 knives and cut the creamy mixture lightly into the potatoes.
- Sprinkle evenly with crushed cornflakes and drizzle with melted butter.
- Bake for 45 minutes.

Serves 12.

Variations: *Leftover mashed potatoes or 4 cups (1 L) frozen hash-brown potatoes can be used instead of grated potatoes.*

Cream of celery or chicken soup can be substituted for cream of mushroom.

Parmesan Baked Potato Wedges

These potatoes go well with fried chicken or steak.

4	baking potatoes	4
	melted butter	
	grated Parmesan cheese	
	seasoning salt	

Parmesan Baked Potato Wedges
Continued

- Preheat oven to 400°F (200°C).
- Wash potatoes, cut into 4 pieces lengthwise.
- Place on a greased baking sheet, skin side down. Brush each piece with melted butter. Sprinkle with Parmesan cheese and seasoning salt.
- Bake for 30 minutes, or until tender. Serve with fried chicken or steak.

Yield: 16 wedges.

Variation: *Dry dillweed is nice sprinkled on top.*

See photograph on page 105.

Orange Sweet Potato Casserole

Great for Christmas dinner. Even those who dislike sweet potatoes will like these.

3 lbs.	sweet potatoes (3½ cups [875 mL] mashed)	1.5 kg
¼ cup	brown sugar	60 mL
2 tbsp.	butter	30 mL
3 tbsp.	frozen orange juice concentrate (undiluted)	45 mL
⅛ tsp.	cinnamon	0.5 mL

Pecan Topping:

⅔ cup	brown sugar	150 mL
⅓ cup	flour	75 mL
1 cup	chopped pecans	250 mL
½ cup	melted butter	125 mL
⅓ cup	flaked coconut	75 mL

- Bake sweet potatoes in oven or microwave until tender.
- If you used the microwave, preheat oven to 350°F (180°C).
- Scoop out the insides; place in a bowl and add brown sugar, butter, orange juice and cinnamon. Mash until well mixed and smooth. A mixer works well.
- Pour into a greased 9" (23 cm) baking dish.
- Mix together all topping ingredients and sprinkle over sweet potatoes. Bake for 20 minutes.
- Remove from oven and serve.

Serves 6-8.

Variation: *Omit pecan topping and top with miniature marshmallows or halved large marshmallows. Bake until lightly browned. This is delicious.*

Outrigger Rice

This is a flavorful dish that goes well with ham or chicken or any sweet and sour dish.

1	small onion, chopped	1
¼ cup	butter OR margarine	60 mL
4 cups	cooked rice	1 L
½ cup	raisins	125 mL
14 oz.	can pineapple tidbits, drained	398 mL
½ tsp.	curry powder	2 mL
1 tsp.	salt	5 mL
½ tsp.	dry tarragon flakes	2 mL

- Preheat oven to 350°F (180°C).
- In a large saucepan, sauté onion in butter until transparent.
- Add remaining ingredients and mix thoroughly.
- Place in a 2-quart (2 L) casserole, cover and bake for 30 minutes.
- Serve with Hawaiian Pork or Chicken, page 110.

Serves 8.

Rice Pilaf

2 cups	chicken broth	500 mL
1	celery stalks, finely diced	1
1 cup	uncooked long-grain OR parboiled rice	250 mL
¼ cup	sliced green onion OR chives	60 mL
⅓ cup	peas	75 mL
3 tbsp.	chopped red pepper	45 mL

- Pour chicken broth into a medium saucepan and add celery and rice.
- Bring to a boil, cover, reduce heat to low and simmer for 10 minutes.
- Remove lid and add green onion, peas and red pepper. Stir in vegetables, cover again and steam for another 10-15 minutes, or until rice is cooked and broth is absorbed.
- Spoon rice into a serving dish and fluff with a fork.

Serves 4-6.

Hint: *An easy way to cook rice is by cooking it as you would for pasta. Boil in plenty of boiling water. When one grain tests "done" after 15-20 minutes, drain rice in a sieve. You will have perfect fluffy rice.*

Stuffed Squash

Q.: What do you call a person who has to buy zucchini at the store?
A: A person who has no friends.

1-2	large zucchini OR yellow crookneck squash	1-2

Herbed Tomato Sauce:

¼ lb.	ground beef	125 g
⅓ cup	minced onion	75 mL
1	small garlic clove, crushed	1
¼ tsp.	salt	1 mL
½ tsp.	pepper	2 mL
7.5 oz.	can tomato sauce	213 mL
1 cup	chicken broth	250 mL
1	bay leaf	1
¼ tsp.	dried oregano	1 mL
¼ tsp.	dried basil	1 mL

Beef and Rice Filling:

1	small onion, chopped	1
1 lb.	ground beef	500 g
	salt and pepper to taste	
1	garlic clove, crushed	1
2	eggs, beaten	2
¼ cup	grated Parmesan cheese	60 mL
⅔ cup	grated Cheddar cheese	150 mL
1 cup	cooked rice	250 mL
½ cup	Tomato Herb Sauce	125 mL

- Slice the squash in half lengthwise and scoop out the flesh and seeds inside, leaving about ¾" (2 cm) rim around the outside.
- Place both halves in a 9 x 13" (23 x 33 cm) baking dish; set aside.
- To prepare sauce, brown ground beef and onion in a heavy skillet. Drain off fat and add remaining ingredients. Cover and simmer over medium heat for 20-30 minutes.
- To prepare filling, brown ground beef and onion. Remove from heat. Drain off fat and stir in remaining ingredients.
- Spoon filling into cavity in squash. Cover all the squash with sauce; bake at 350°F (180°C), covered, for 45 minutes or 1 hour, until squash is cooked.
- Garnish with Parmesan cheese or grated Cheddar.
- Serve with French bread and Caesar salad, page 75.

Serves 6-8.

Cheater's Baked Beans

These taste just like you've slaved in the kitchen for a couple of days.
They taste like homemade from scratch.

3 x 14 oz.	cans beans with pork	3 x 398 mL
1	large onion, chopped	1
1	green pepper, chopped	1
½ cup	ketchup	125 mL
14 oz.	can crushed pineapple, drained	398 mL
⅓ cup	brown sugar	75 mL
¼ cup	molasses	60 mL
1½ tsp.	Worcestershire sauce	7 mL
½ lb.	lean bacon, fried and chopped	250 g

- In a large mixing bowl, combine all ingredients.
- Pour into a 3-quart (3 L) casserole.
- Cover and bake at 325°F (160°C) for 2 hours.
- Remove cover and bake for 30 minutes more, stirring occasionally.

Serves 8.

Creamy Green Beans

These are quick and easy to make and delicious. A convenience recipe that you
can always have on hand.

3 cups	French-style frozen green beans	750 mL
1	small onion, sliced	1
2 tbsp.	butter	30 mL
10 oz.	can mushroom soup, undiluted OR Mushroom Sauce, page 66	284 mL
10 oz.	can water chestnuts, drained and sliced	284 mL
10 oz.	can sliced mushrooms	284 mL

- Preheat oven to 350°F (180°C).
- Blanch green beans in boiling water and drain.
- Fry onion in butter until transparent.
- In a 2-quart (2 L) casserole, combine all ingredients and stir well to coat.
- Cover and bake for 20 minutes.

Serves 6-8.

Variations: *Add ¼ cup (60 mL) roasted slivered almonds. Dry chow mein noodles are very good sprinkled on top of beans 5 minutes before removing from oven.*

Green Beans with Honey-Lemon Sauce

This is a nice tangy sauce that complements the flavor of the beans.

1 lb.	fresh green beans	500 g
2 tbsp.	lemon juice	30 mL
2 tbsp.	honey	30 mL
1 tbsp.	butter	15 mL
1	garlic clove, crushed	1

- Cut beans in half. Place in a saucepan with about 1" (2.5 cm) water and boil, or steam in a steamer, until tender-crisp, about 5 minutes. DO NOT OVERCOOK.
- Meanwhile, prepare honey-lemon sauce.
- In a small saucepan, combine lemon juice, honey and butter. Bring to a boil and simmer for 2 minutes over medium heat.
- Add crushed garlic and simmer for 30 seconds.
- Remove garlic and discard.
- Drain water off beans and pour beans into a serving bowl.
- Pour honey-lemon sauce over beans and toss to coat.
- Serve immediately as a side dish with any type of meat.

Serves 6.

Variation: This sauce is also very good over steamed broccoli.

See photograph on page 105.

*Even if you are on the right track,
you will get run over if you just stand there.
(Arthur Godfrey)*

Harvard Beets

This is an excellent way to serve fresh beets from the garden.

2 cups	diced OR sliced cooked beets	500 mL
2 tbsp.	butter	30 mL
2 tbsp.	flour	30 mL
¼ cup	boiling water	60 mL
3 tbsp.	vinegar	45 mL
⅓ cup	brown sugar	75 mL
⅛ tsp.	ground cloves	0.5 mL
⅛ tsp.	ground cinnamon	0.5 mL
¼ tsp.	salt	1 mL

- Cook beets, drain and dice. Transfer to a bowl.
- In the beet pot, melt butter and stir in flour.
- Add remaining ingredients and whisk together. Stir over medium heat until bubbly.
- Pour over beets and toss to coat.
- Serve warm as a side dish.

Serves 4.

*A second-grade teacher who had given a lesson on magnets
asked her class the following test question:
"What starts with 'M' and picks up things?"
Many of the children wrote "Mother".*

Pasta

Creamy Parmesan Fusilli, page 92
Deluxe Spinach Salad, page 74

Casseroles
&
Main Dishes

Macaroni and Cheese

This is the creamiest macaroni you'll ever make.

Base:

1½ cups	uncooked macaroni	375 mL
¼ cup	butter OR margarine	60 mL
¼ cup	flour	60 mL
2 cups	milk	500 mL
1 tsp.	salt	5 mL
1 tsp.	sugar	5 mL
3 tbsp.	processed cheese spread	45 mL
½ lb.	grated sharp Cheddar cheese	250 g
½ cup	sour cream	125 mL
1½ cups	cottage cheese	375 mL

Topping:

2 cups	grated mild OR medium Cheddar cheese	500 mL
1½ cups	soft fine bread crumbs	375 mL
¼ cup	butter OR margarine, melted	60 mL

- Cook macaroni according to directions on package. Drain.
- In a large pot, melt butter and add flour to make a paste.
- Add milk a little at a time, stirring or whisking constantly.
- Add remaining ingredients and cook until bubbly and thick.
- Stir in cooked macaroni and pour into a 9 x 13" (23 x 33 cm) greased pan. This will be runny but it thickens as it bakes.
- Preheat oven to 350°F (180°C).
- Combine topping ingredients and sprinkle over macaroni.
- Bake for 30 minutes, uncovered.

Serves 10.

Russian Lasagne

This is an adaptation of a recipe I got from my friend Sandy who often brings this casserole to potluck suppers. It goes over very well. This tastes just like perogies only it is easier to make.

9	lasagne noodles	9
2 cups	creamed cottage cheese	500 mL
1/4 cup	grated Parmesan cheese	60 mL
1	egg, lightly beaten	1
1/4 tsp.	onion salt	1 mL
2 cups	mashed potatoes (don't add butter or milk)	500 mL
1 1/4 cups	grated medium Cheddar cheese	300 mL
1/4 cup	sour cream	60 mL
1 tbsp.	thinly sliced green onion OR chives	15 mL
1/4 tsp.	salt	1 mL
1/4 tsp.	onion salt	1 mL
1/4 tsp.	pepper	1 mL
6	slices bacon, chopped and fried until crisp (reserve 1 tbsp. [15 mL] of grease)	6
1	medium onion, chopped	1
1/2 cup	butter OR margarine, melted	125 mL
	sour cream for garnish	

- Cook lasagne noodles according to package directions and drain.
- Place 3 noodles lengthwise in the bottom of a lightly greased 9 x 13" (23 x 33 cm) pan.
- Mix cottage cheese, grated Parmesan cheese, egg and onion salt together and spread over noodles in pan.
- Place 3 more noodles over cottage cheese mixture.
- Combine mashed potatoes, Cheddar cheese, sour cream, chives and remaining seasonings. Spread over second layer of noodles.
- Place 3 more noodles on top of potato mixture.
- Sprinkle fried bacon over noodles.
- Preheat oven to 350°F (180°C).
- Fry chopped onion in butter and reserved bacon grease until onion is translucent. Pour evenly over casserole. Cover with foil and bake for 30 minutes.
- Remove from oven and let sit for 10 minutes before slicing.
- Serve with sour cream on the side for garnish and a green salad.

Yield: 6-8 servings.

Variation: *Try 1/4 cup (60 mL) drained sauerkraut in potato mixture instead of sour cream.*

Creamy Parmesan Fusilli

If you're a pasta lover, this dish will disappear quickly. This is a favorite recipe. My husband created it after eating it at a popular Edmonton Italian restaurant.

4 cups	uncooked fusilli OR rotini	1 L
3 tbsp.	butter	45 mL
2/3 cup	Parmesan cheese	150 mL
1/3 cup	snipped fresh parsley	75 mL
1 1/2 tbsp.	mayonnaise	22 mL
1/2 cup	whipping cream	125 mL
1	garlic clove, minced	1
8	bacon slices, fried crisp and crumbled	8
	pepper to taste	

- Cook pasta according to directions on pasta package and drain.
- While pasta is cooking prepare the sauce.
- Melt butter in saucepan.
- Add Parmesan cheese, parsley, mayonnaise, cream and garlic. Mix well and warm thoroughly. Do not let this boil.
- Toss cheese mixture with hot pasta and crumbled bacon until pasta is well coated.
- Season to taste with pepper and serve immediately.
- Have additional Parmesan cheese on the table for those who might like more.

Serves 4.

Variations: *Toss with 2-3 tbsp. (30-45 mL) sliced, pitted ripe or green olives.*

Add 3 oz. (85 g) sliced fresh mushrooms to cheese mixture.

Serve sliced tomatoes on the side.

Add finely diced sun-dried tomatoes to the cheese mixture prior to tossing with pasta.

Crab Fusilli or Linguine: *Substitute 1/2 lb. (250 g) of flaked crab meat for the bacon. Use either fusilli or linguine noodles.*

See photograph on page 87.

Pizza Sauce

This sauce is nice and thick.

1	small onion, minced (½ cup [125 mL])	1
2 tbsp.	oil	30 mL
¼ cup	water	60 mL
14 oz.	can crushed tomatoes	398 mL
¼ tsp.	ground thyme	1 mL
1 tsp.	dry basil flakes	5 mL
½ tsp.	dry oregano flakes	2 mL
½ tsp.	tarragon	2 mL
¼ tsp.	coarsely ground black pepper	1 mL
1	small garlic clove, crushed	1
1 tsp.	sugar	5 mL
½ tsp.	chili powder	2 mL
½ tsp.	Worcestershire sauce	2 mL

- In a small skillet, sauté onion in oil until translucent. Transfer to a small saucepan.
- Add remaining ingredients and stir until well mixed.
- Simmer over medium-low heat for 20 minutes.
- Stir occasionally.

Yield: 2 cups (500 mL), enough for 2 large pizzas.

Variation: *For extra spicy sauce add 2 tbsp. (30 mL) hot salsa.*

He who slings mud loses ground.

Pizza

Instead of ordering "take out" try making your own.
You will receive great applause for this one.

Crust:

1⅓ cups	warm water	325 mL
1 tbsp.	sugar	15 mL
1 tsp.	salt	5 mL
1	egg	1
2 tbsp.	oil	30 mL
1 tbsp.	yeast	15 mL
3½ cups	flour (approximately)	875 mL
	Italian tomato sauce OR pizza sauce, page 93	
	mozzarella cheese, shredded	
	toppings, page 95	

- In a medium-sized bowl, whisk together water, sugar, salt, egg and oil.
- Sprinkle yeast over liquid in bowl and let stand 5 minutes.
- Stir in flour a little at a time, until you have a smooth but firm dough.
- Knead in the last ½ cup (125 mL) flour.
- Let rise until double in bulk. Punch down. Divide dough into 2 pieces. Let rise 10 more minutes.
- Place dough on 2 large greased pizza pans. Spread dough with fingers and pinch dough around the edges of the pan to make a lip.
- Spread with sauce to the edges.
- Sprinkle liberally with mozzarella cheese and toppings of your choice. Sprinkle a bit more cheese over toppings.
- Bake at 400°F (200°C) for 25-30 minutes, or until crust is golden brown on the bottom and cheese is melted and bubbly. Put one pan in center of oven and one pan on bottom rack. Switch halfway through baking.
- This dough can be frozen for use at a later date. Just thaw before ready to use. It can be frozen in the pizza pan too. Just thaw and bake.

Yield: 2 large pizzas.

Variations: *Sprinkle pan with cornmeal, sesame seeds or poppy seeds before spreading dough.*

Pizza

Continued

Try these topping combinations:

Mozzarella cheese mixed with Monterey Jack cheese.

Ham, pineapple, green pepper.

Pepperoni, mushroom and jalapeño peppers.

Shrimp, tomato and sliced black olives.

Shrimp, feta cheese, sliced black olives and red and green peppers.

Broccoli florets, snow peas, asparagus spears and shrimp or crab.

Bacon and tomato.

Loaded, with all of the above.

Pizza Burritos

6	flour tortillas, page 15, precooked	6
	pizza sauce, page 93, OR 2 cups (500 mL)	
	canned pizza sauce	
	grated mozzarella cheese	

Pizza Toppers:

ham, pineapple, green pepper, mushrooms, pepperoni, shrimp, also see suggestions above

- Place a tortilla on a plate; thinly spread with sauce.
- Sprinkle with mozzarella cheese.
- Add desired toppings.
- Broil or microwave on high until cheese melts, about 1 minute.
- Roll up like a burrito. Remember to tuck in the bottom and fold both sides over the filling so you have a leakproof (hopefully) package.

Yield: 6 Burritos.

Fajitas (Fah-hee-tahs)

This is basically a Mexican stir-fry dish wrapped in a tortilla.

6	cooked, warm flour tortillas, page 15	6
2 tbsp.	vegetable oil	30 mL
1 lb.	sirloin steak, thinly sliced, OR pork OR chicken	500 g
1	onion, halved, sliced in thin strips	1
1	green pepper, seeded, cut in thin strips	1
⅛ tsp.	pepper	0.5 mL
½ tsp.	chili powder	2 mL
5 drops	Tabasco sauce	5 drops
¼ tsp.	cumin	1 mL
¼ tsp.	salt	1 mL
2	tomatoes, seeded, sliced in thin strips	2
1 cup	grated Cheddar cheese	250 mL
	lettuce thinly sliced	
	salsa	
	sour cream	

- Have tortillas ready.
- In a skillet, heat the oil and stir-fry meat, onions and green pepper until cooked.
- Sprinkle on seasonings and stir.
- Quickly add tomatoes and toss to mix.
- Remove from heat.
- Put a tortilla on a plate. Spoon ⅙ of the fried mixture down the middle of the tortilla.
- Sprinkle on cheese and lettuce.
- Spoon 1 tbsp. (15 mL) salsa evenly over filling.
- Top with sour cream if desired.
- Roll up tightly and eat.

Serves 6.

Variations: *Salsa can be put on the outside instead of the inside. Sweet red pepper or yellow pepper can be used instead of green pepper or use both.*

Crispy Fried Fish Fillets

This coating is excellent with pickerel, perch, pike or any white-fleshed lakefish.

1 cup	crushed cornflakes	250 mL
2	2" (5 cm) square soda crackers, crushed	2
¼ cup	flour	60 mL
¼ cup	cornmeal	60 mL
½ tsp.	salt	2 mL
½ tsp.	lemon pepper	2 mL
¼ cup	milk	60 mL
1	egg	1
	vegetable oil	
2 lbs.	fish fillets (pickerel, perch OR pike)	1 kg

- In a blender or food processor, blend cornflakes, crackers, flour, cornmeal, salt and lemon pepper until mixture becomes fine crumbs. Pour into a shallow dish and spread evenly.
- In a small bowl, beat milk and egg together.
- Put enough oil, in a deep skillet to cover the bottom ½" (1.3 cm) deep. Heat to 375°F (190°C) or when the tip of a wooden spoon dipped in the oil quickly produces a lot of sizzling bubbles.
- Dip fish into egg mixture.
- Coat with crumbs. Place in hot oil.
- Fry on both sides until golden brown.
- Check to see if fish is completely cooked, with no translucent flesh remaining.
- Place on paper toweling.
- Serve with tartar sauce.

Serves 4.

Quick Tartar Sauce

½ cup	mayonnaise	125 mL
1 tbsp.	sweet pickle relish	15 mL
1 tsp.	lemon juice	5 mL

- Combine all ingredients.

Salmon with Blueberry Sauce

I was served a similar dish in a restaurant in Toronto.
It was soooo good that I came home and recreated it.

4	salmon steaks	4
1 cup	fresh OR frozen blueberries	250 mL
¼ cup	sugar	60 mL
1 tbsp.	vinegar	15 mL
¼ cup	butter	60 mL
½ tsp.	lemon pepper	2 mL

- Thaw salmon if frozen.
- In a small saucepan, combine blueberries, sugar and vinegar.
- Bring to boil over medium-high heat and continue with a rolling boil for 4 minutes, stirring and crushing the berries.
- Remove from heat. Set aside but keep warm.
- Preheat broiler or barbecue.
- Melt butter in a small saucepan. Stir in lemon pepper.
- Over a barbecue grill or under a broiler (6" [15 cm] from heat) broil salmon for about 5-7 minutes on each side, until fish flakes when tested with a fork.
- Brush with lemon butter while grilling.
- Serve with blueberry sauce on top or put sauce in a side dish and dip forkfuls of salmon in the blueberry sauce.
- Serve with a green salad and rice.

Serves 4.

See photograph on page 105.

It's impossible to push yourself ahead
by patting yourself on the back.

Chicken Broccoli Casserole

Variations of this delicious casserole have been popular for many years.

2-3	chicken breasts	2-3
5 cups	chopped broccoli (2 lbs. [1 kg]) stems and florets	1.25 L
10 oz.	can cream of chicken OR cream of celery soup (undiluted) OR 1 cup (250 mL) Basic Low-Cal Sauce, page 66	284 mL
1 cup	milk	250 mL
½ cup	sour cream OR plain yogurt	125 mL
½ cup	mayonnaise	125 mL
1 tbsp.	lemon juice	15 mL
1 cup	grated Cheddar cheese	250 mL
⅔ cup	buttered bread crumbs	150 mL

- Simmer chicken breasts in lightly salted water until juice runs clear.
- Remove chicken from water, skin and bone.
- Cut chicken in bite-sized pieces and distribute evenly on the bottom of a 9" (23 cm) square pan.
- Wash broccoli and remove the woody outer skin of the stems. Chop broccoli into bite-sized pieces.
- Scatter broccoli over chicken pieces.
- Combine soup, milk, sour cream, mayonnaise and lemon juice, and whisk until smooth.
- Stir in cheese.
- Pour cheese mixture over broccoli and chicken.
- Cover with foil and bake at 350°F (180°C) for 30 minutes.
- Sprinkle with buttered bread crumbs.
- Bake for 10 minutes more, uncovered.
- Remove from oven and serve with rice.

Serves 6.

Chicken À La King In a Puff Shell

An elegant way to serve Chicken à la King.

Filling:

¼ cup	butter OR margarine	60 mL
½ cup	diced onion	125 mL
⅓ cup	flour	75 mL
½ tsp.	salt	2 mL
¼ tsp.	pepper	1 mL
1 cup	chicken broth	250 mL
1 cup	milk	250 mL
2 cups	chopped cooked chicken	500 mL
10 oz.	can mushroom pieces and stems, drained	298 mL
½ cup	peas	125 mL
1	medium carrot, diced and parboiled	1

Puff Shell Mixture:

1 cup	boiling water	250 mL
½ cup	butter OR margarine	125 mL
1 cup	flour	250 mL
4	eggs	4
½ cup	grated cheese	125 mL
2 tsp.	dried parsley flakes OR 2 tbsp. (30 mL) chopped fresh parsley	10 mL
⅛ tsp.	salt	0.5 mL

- In a heavy saucepan, melt butter and add onion.
- Sauté until onion is translucent.
- Stir in flour, salt and pepper until evenly blended.
- Add chicken broth and milk. Stir with a whisk to blend. Then stir with a spoon over medium-heat until thick and bubbly.
- Add chicken, drained mushrooms, peas and diced carrot.
- Heat, stirring constantly, until carrots are cooked.
- Keep warm until puff shells are ready.

Chicken À La King In a Puff Shell

Continued

Puff Shells

- In a medium-sized, heavy saucepan, boil water and butter together over medium heat until butter is completely melted.
- Add flour all at once and continue to cook over medium heat stirring constantly. The mixture will form a ball in the pan. Remove from heat.
- Cool for 5 minutes.
- Preheat oven to 425°F (220°C).
- Add eggs 1 at a time, beating well after each addition.
- Spoon batter into greased muffin cups.
- Bake for 25-30 minutes, or until puffy on the outside and hollow in the middle.
- Remove puffs from oven. Split in half; pour Chicken À La King into each puff.
- Serve with a green salad.

Yield: 10 puff shells; serves 10.

Variation: *For Chicken À La King Crêpes see instructions on page 11.*

Work done by the hour is tedious.
Work done by the job is interesting.

Turkey Pie

An excellent and tasty way to use up leftover turkey.
Make some pies now and freeze the rest for a busy night.
I guarantee you will not find a better turkey pie recipe.

¾ cup	butter	175 mL
¾ cup	chopped onion	175 mL
½ cup	thinly sliced celery	125 mL
1 cup	flour	250 mL
1½ tsp.	salt	7 mL
6 cups	chicken broth	1.5 L
4	large carrots, peeled and thinly sliced	4
2 cups	frozen peas	500 mL
7 cups	chopped cooked turkey	1.75 L
	pastry recipe, page 174	

- In a large pot, heat butter and sauté onion and celery until tender.
- Stir in flour and salt until blended evenly.
- Pour in broth all at once and whisk thoroughly.
- Cook, stirring constantly, until thick and bubbly.
- Add carrots, peas and turkey.
- Cook until carrots are tender-crisp, about 8-10 minutes.
- Pour into 2, 9" (23 cm) pie plates or 12 individual pie pans.
- Roll out prepared pastry ¼" (1 cm) thick and cut to fit tops of pie plates.
- Cut a couple of slits with a knife in middle of the pastry.
  At this point you can freeze for use at a later date. Cover tightly with foil and place in freezer.
- Preheat oven to 400°F (200°C).
- Place pies on baking sheets to catch drips.
- Bake, uncovered, in oven until pastry is golden brown, approximately 15 minutes, or 20 minutes for frozen pies.

Serves 12.

Variation: *Reduce turkey by 2 cups (500 mL) and add 2 large potatoes, cubed.*

Hint: *Precook carrots and potatoes before adding to gravy mixture.*

Chicken Chow Mein

This is a delicious and nutritious dish. It has great color and flavor.

⅔ cup	chopped onion	150 mL
¼ cup	butter OR margarine	60 mL
2 cups	bias-sliced celery	500 mL
1 cup	thinly sliced carrots	250 mL
1	small bunch broccoli, finely chopped	1
2 cups	fresh bean sprouts	500 mL
2 cups	thinly sliced cabbage	500 mL
10 oz.	can water chestnuts, sliced (reserve liquid)	284 mL
10 oz.	can sliced mushrooms (reserve liquid)	284 mL
2-3 cups	cooked chicken, turkey OR pork	500-750 mL
2 cups	liquid (from water chestnuts and mushrooms plus water)	500 mL
⅓ cup	flour	75 mL
3 tbsp.	soy sauce	45 mL
1 tsp.	salt	5 mL
¼ tsp.	pepper	1 mL
	chow mein noodles (dry type)	

- Preheat oven to 325°F (160°C).
- Sauté onions in butter until transparent.
- Add celery, carrots and broccoli and cook until tender crisp.
- Add bean sprouts, cabbage, chicken, water chestnuts and mushrooms. Stir lightly to mix.
- Combine cold liquid, flour, soy sauce and seasonings.
- Add to chicken/vegetable mixture. Cook and stir until liquid thickens and coats vegetables.
- Pour into a 9 x 13" (23 x 33 cm) pan.
- Sprinkle with chow mein noodles.
- Bake for 10-15 minutes.
- Serve with rice.

Serves 6.

Variations: *Turkey, pork or beef can be used instead of chicken.*

Chicken Cordon Bleu

Entertaining at its best. Impress your guests with this elegant gourmet dish.

3	boneless whole chicken breasts, 6 halves	3
6	thin slices of ham	6
6	thin slices of Swiss cheese OR finely grated Swiss cheese	6
¼ cup	flour	60 mL
½ tsp.	seasoned salt	2 mL
¼ tsp.	each salt and pepper	1 mL
1	egg, beaten	1
2 tbsp.	milk	30 mL
⅓ cup	dried bread crumbs	75 mL
⅓ cup	cornflake crumbs	75 mL
¼ cup	oil	60 mL
¼ cup	water	60 mL

- Pound each chicken breast half to ¼" (1 cm) thickness.
- Place a piece of ham then a piece of cheese on top of each chicken breast.
- Roll up breast, tucking in loose ends. Secure with 1 or 2 toothpicks.
- Mix flour with seasonings and coat each roll with seasoned flour mixture.
- Beat egg and milk together in a bowl.
- Combine crumbs together in another bowl.
- Dip flour-coated chicken in egg mixture then roll in crumbs until thoroughly coated.
- Heat oil in a deep skillet.
- Brown rolls on all sides in hot oil. Pour water into skillet all at once. Cover with a lid and simmer for 40 minutes over medium heat.
- Preheat oven to 350°F (180°C).
- Transfer rolls to a greased shallow pan. Bake, uncovered, for 10 minutes.
- Serve with Cordon Bleu Sauce below.

Yield: 6 servings.

Cordon Bleu Sauce

1 cup	Basic Low-Cal Sauce, page 66	250 mL
½ cup	sour cream	125 mL
¼ cup	grated Swiss cheese	60 mL
¼ cup	milk OR water	60 mL
1 tsp.	lemon juice	5 mL

- In a small saucepan, whisk all ingredients together and heat over medium heat until hot. Pour over Chicken Cordon Bleu.

Fish

Salmon with Blueberry Sauce, page 98
Green Beans with Honey Lemon Sauce, page 85
Parmesan Baked Potato Wedges, page 80

Crispy Oven-Fried Chicken

Instead of buying commercial coating mixes try making your own.
You will be impressed with the results.

½ cup	flour (all-purpose OR whole-wheat)	125 mL
¼ cup	bread, cornflake OR cracker crumbs	60 mL
1 tbsp.	paprika	5 mL
½-1 tsp.	salt	2-5 mL
2 tsp.	baking powder	10 mL
½ tsp.	seasoning salt	2 mL
¼ tsp.	onion powder	1 mL
⅛ tsp.	garlic powder	0.5 mL
¼ tsp.	black pepper	1 mL
¼ tsp.	poultry seasoning	1 mL
1 tsp.	sugar	5 mL
1 tsp.	instant chicken bouillon granules	5 mL
1	egg	1
½ cup	milk	125 mL
12	pieces of chicken	12
¼-½ cup	melted butter	60-125 mL

- Preheat oven to 350°F (180°C).
- In a blender or food processor, combine all the dry ingredients. Blend until evenly mixed.
- Transfer to a bag or bowl.
- In a small bowl, whisk together egg and milk.
- Dip chicken pieces 1 at a time into egg and milk mixture.
- Drop into crumb mixture and coat evenly by shaking in a bag or turning in crumb mix in bowl.
- Place on greased baking sheet.
- Drizzle with melted butter.
- Bake for 45-55 minutes, until chicken is cooked.

Serves 6.

Variation: *Instead of dipping chicken pieces in a mixture of egg and milk, use ½-¾ cup (125-175 mL) plain yogurt.*

Buffalo Wings

You're right, Buffalo don't have wings. This comes right from Buffalo, New York.

3 lbs.	chicken wings	1.5 kg
½ cup	apricot jam	125 mL
1¼ oz.	pkg. dry onion soup	35 g
1 cup	Catalina salad dressing	250 mL
5 drops	Tabasco sauce	5 drops

- Roast wings in oven, covered, at 350°F (180°C) for 30 minutes.
- Drain off fat.
- Mix remaining ingredients in a small saucepan and bring to a boil over medium heat. Simmer for about 2-3 minutes and remove from stove.
- Brush sauce over wings. Bake about 15-20 minutes longer, or until tender.

Serves 6-8.

Variations: *This sauce is great on any chicken pieces, also on spareribs.*

Honey Barbecued Chicken

This is delicious served with the Deluxe Spinach Salad, page 74.

1	chicken, cut up	1
¾ cup	ketchup	175 mL
2 tbsp.	lemon juice	30 mL
1 tsp.	Worcestershire sauce	5 mL
¼ cup	honey	60 mL
¼ cup	brown sugar	60 mL
1 tbsp.	prepared mustard	15 mL
⅛ tsp.	pepper	0.5 mL
5 drops	Louisiana hot sauce	5 drops

- Bake chicken pieces, covered, in a 375°F (190°C) oven for 35 minutes.
- To make barbecue sauce, combine remaining ingredients and set aside.
- Remove cover from baked chicken and drain off liquid.
- Spoon sauce over chicken and bake, uncovered, for 20 more minutes, basting every 5 minutes.
- Remove from oven and serve.

Serves 5.

Variation: *Try pork spareribs instead of chicken.*

Blender Barbecue Sauce

Use this versatile sauce on chicken, pork or beef.

1 cup	ketchup	250 mL
1 tbsp.	lemon juice	15 mL
1 tbsp.	vinegar	15 mL
¼ cup	water	60 mL
½ cup	minced onion	125 mL
1	garlic clove, minced	1
1 tbsp.	Worcestershire sauce	15 mL
3 tbsp.	brown sugar	45 mL

- Put everything into the blender and blend until smooth.
- Use immediately or store in the refrigerator.

Yield: 1⅔ cups (400 mL).

Sweet and Sour Spareribs

2 lbs.	pork ribs	1 kg
	salt and pepper to taste	
½ cup	brown sugar	125 mL
¼ cup	vinegar	60 mL
¼ cup	ketchup	60 mL
14 oz.	can pineapple tidbits	398 mL
1 tbsp.	soy sauce	15 mL
2 tbsp.	cornstarch	30 mL
½ cup	cold water	125 mL

- Slice ribs into individual pieces. Place in a 9 x 13" (23 x 33 cm) pan or 2-quart (2 L) casserole.
- Sprinkle with salt and pepper.
- Bake, covered, at 375°F (190°C) for 40 minutes, or until done. Lower oven temperature to 350°F (180°C).
- Drain off fat.
- Mix brown sugar, vinegar, ketchup, pineapple and soy sauce together.
- Stir cornstarch into cold water and add to sugar and vinegar mixture. Stir until well mixed. Pour over drained spareribs.
- Cover and bake for 30-40 minutes, or until thick and bubbly.
- Serve over rice.

Serves 6.

Hawaiian Pork

When I was growing up, my mother prepared this recipe on special occasions.

| 1 lb. | pork shoulder roast, cut in 1" (2.5 cm) cubes | 500 g |
| | oil for deep frying | |

Batter:

6	eggs	6
1 tsp.	salt	5 mL
½ tsp.	baking powder	2 mL
¾ cup	flour	175 mL

Sauce:

19 oz.	can pineapple chunks, not drained	540 mL
2½ cups	chicken broth	625 mL
⅓ cup	vinegar	75 mL
⅔ cup	brown sugar	150 mL
1 tbsp.	soy sauce	15 mL
2	green peppers, cut in 1" (2.5 cm) squares	2
½ cup	cold water	125 mL
⅓ cup	cornstarch	75 mL

- Cut pork into 1" (2.5 cm) cubes.
- In a deep-fryer or electric frying pan, heat oil to 375°F (190°C).
- While oil is heating, make a batter in a medium-sized bowl by combining eggs, salt, baking powder and flour until smooth.
- Add pork, a little at a time, to batter. Coat thoroughly.
- With a small spoon, place batter-dipped pork into hot oil.
- When batter is a deep golden brown, turn pork over and cook the other side.
- Remove pork from hot oil and drain on paper towels. Make sure pork is cooked, then set aside. This can be made 1 day ahead and refrigerated.
- In a medium-sized saucepan, combine pineapple (juice and all), chicken broth, vinegar, brown sugar, soy sauce and green peppers. Simmer until green pepper is cooked, about 15 minutes.
- Combine cold water and cornstarch. Stir into hot sauce; cook until thick.
- Place pork fritters into a large deep casserole and pour sauce over.
- Cover and bake at 350°F (180°C) for 30 minutes.
- Serve over rice.

Serves 8.

Variation:

Hawaiian Chicken: *Bake or fry 4 lbs. (2 kg) of chicken pieces. Drain off fat; pour sauce over, cover and bake at 350°F (180°C) for 30 minutes.*

Chinese Beef with Broccoli

2 tbsp.	oil	30 mL
1 lb.	sirloin OR flank steak, sliced in thin strips	500 g
1/2	medium onion, thinly sliced	1/2
1/4 lb.	sliced fresh mushrooms (optional)	115 g
4 cups	small broccoli florets	1 L
1/4 tsp.	salt	1 mL
	pepper to taste	
1	small garlic clove, crushed	1
3 tbsp.	water	45 mL
1/2 cup	cold water	125 mL
3 tbsp.	cornstarch	45 mL
2 tsp.	sugar	10 mL
1 cup	beef broth	250 mL
2 tbsp.	soy sauce	30 mL

- In a deep skillet, heat the oil, add the beef and onions and brown over medium-high heat until beef is cooked and onion is transparent.
- Add mushrooms, broccoli and seasonings.
- Stir-fry until evenly distributed in pan.
- Add 3 tbsp. (45 mL) water and cover.
- Simmer for 2-3 minutes, or until broccoli is tender-crisp.
- Mix the 1/2 cup (125 mL) cold water and cornstarch until cornstarch is dissolved.
- Add remaining ingredients to cornstarch mixture.
- Pour over meat and vegetables and stir until sauce is thick and vegetables are coated.
- Add more water if you prefer a thinner sauce.
- Serve with steamed rice.

Serves 4-6.

Variation: Use this recipe, without the broccoli, in Beef Stroganoff Crêpes, page 11.

Note: Slice beef when partially frozen. It can be sliced thinner this way.

Barbecued Beef On A Bun

*This is a recipe from my sister, Margo, who serves it at family get-togethers.
An easy meal for a crowd of folks after skiing or any all-day outing.
It cooks while you are out having fun.*

2½-3 lbs.	beef roast (any inexpensive cut will do)	1.25-1.5 kg
1 tbsp.	instant beef bouillon granules	15 mL
1	onion, chopped	1
½	green pepper, diced	½
1	celery stalk, diced	1
¼ tsp.	ground black pepper	1 mL
7½ oz.	can tomato sauce	213 mL
1 cup	barbecue sauce	250 mL
½ cup	brown sugar	125 mL
	buns	

- Place roast in a large crock pot (slow cooker).
- Sprinkle beef bouillon granules, onion, green pepper, celery and black pepper over roast.
- Cover with lid and cook for at least 8 hours. Do not add any liquid to this.
- After roast has cooked for 8 hours combine tomato sauce, barbecue sauce and brown sugar and pour over beef.
- Stir. Beef should be tender enough to break into chunks.
- Bake in slow cooker 1 more hour.
- Serve beef on buns, with a green salad on the side.
- Deluxe Spinach Salad, page 74, goes very well with this dish.

Serves 8-10.

Variation: *A 1¼ oz. (35 g) pkg. of dry onion soup can be substituted for onion and beef bouillon granules.*

Note: *If you don't have a slow cooker, bake at 225-250°F (107-120°C) for 8 hours.*

Swiss Steak

This is a good "stick to-the-ribs" entrée for those cold winter evenings.

2 lbs.	chuck OR round steak	1 kg
2 tbsp.	oil	30 mL
¾ cup	chopped onion	175 mL
1	celery stalk, thinly sliced	1
¼ cup	chopped green pepper	60 mL
19 oz.	can tomatoes, chopped	540 mL
½ tsp.	black pepper	2 mL
1 tsp.	Worcestershire sauce	5 mL
1½ cups	V-8 juice (reserve ½ cup [125 mL] for thickening)	375 mL
3 tbsp.	flour	45 mL
¼ cup	cold water	60 mL

- Cut steak into 6 pieces.
- In a skillet, over medium heat, brown steak in oil.
- Remove steak and place in a 9 x 13" (23 x 33 cm) pan.
- Preheat oven to 350°F (180°C).
- In the same skillet, sauté onion, celery and green pepper until tender.
- Add tomatoes, black pepper, Worcestershire sauce and 1 cup (250 mL) of the V-8 juice. Bring to a boil and pour over steak.
- Cover pan and bake for 1 hour.
- Reduce heat to 300°F (150°C) and bake for 45 minutes.
- In a measuring cup, mix ½ cup (125 mL) V-8 juice, water and flour, whisking together until smooth.
- Stir into sauce evenly. Bake 10 more minutes at 350°F (180°C).
- Serve with mashed potatoes and green salad.

Serves 6.

Chili Con Carne

This is even better reheated the next day.

1½ lbs.	ground beef	750 g
1	large onion, chopped	1
1	large green pepper, chopped	1
28 oz.	can tomatoes, chopped	796 mL
14 oz.	can kidney beans, drained and rinsed	398 mL
14 oz.	can beans with pork	398 mL
10 oz.	can sliced mushrooms	284 mL
5.5 oz.	can tomato paste	156 mL
½ cup	water	125 mL
½ lb.	bacon, fried crisp and crumbled	250 g
½ tsp.	cumin	2 mL
1-2 tbsp.	chili powder	15-30 mL
½ tsp.	black pepper	2 mL
½ tsp.	salt	2 mL
1	garlic clove, crushed	1
¼ tsp.	cayenne (optional, if you like it hot)	1 mL

- Brown ground beef in a skillet and drain off fat.
- Sauté onion and green pepper with ground beef until tender.
- Transfer to a large pot, slow cooker or casserole.
- Stir in remaining ingredients.
- Simmer for at least 2 hours, at 325°F (160°C) in the oven or over medium-low heat on the stove top or for 6 hours in a slow cooker.
- Serve with freshly baked buns and a green salad.

Serves 8-10.

Minds are like parachutes,
they only function when opened.

Make-Ahead Enchilada Casserole

This is excellent for potluck dinners.

1½ lbs.	lean ground beef	750 g
1	medium onion, chopped	1
1	green pepper, chopped	1
19 oz.	can tomatoes, diced	540 mL
5.5 oz.	can tomato paste	156 mL
1 cup	hot taco sauce	250 mL
14 oz.	can kidney OR pinto beans, drained, rinsed	398 mL
12 oz.	can whole kernel corn, drained	341 mL
2 tbsp.	mild chili powder	30 mL
¼ tsp.	salt	1 mL
½ tsp.	ground black pepper	2 mL
½ tsp.	cumin (optional)	2 mL
1 cup	grated mild OR medium Cheddar cheese	250 mL
4 cups	broken corn chips	1 L

Toppings:

2 cups	sour cream	500 mL
1	ripe avocado, peeled and chopped (optional)	1
1	large tomato, seeded and chopped	1
1 cup	grated mild OR medium Cheddar cheese	250 mL
1½ cups	shredded lettuce	375 mL
1	green, red OR yellow pepper, chopped	1
½ cup	sliced pitted black olives	125 mL
1 cup	broken corn chips	250 mL

- In a large deep skillet, brown ground beef over medium heat. Drain off fat.
- Add onion and green pepper and sauté until they are cooked.
- Pour in tomatoes, tomato paste and taco sauce. Stir until evenly mixed.
- Add kidney beans, corn and seasonings. Simmer for 5 minutes.
- Remove from heat. Stir in cheese and corn chips until evenly mixed.
- Pour into a greased 9 x 13" (23 x 33 cm) pan. Spread evenly.
- Cover and refrigerate for 3 hours or overnight.
- Remove from refrigerator, cover with foil. Bake at 350°F (180°C) for 40 minutes, or until piping hot.
- Remove from oven and just before serving spread with sour cream. Assemble toppings in order given over top of casserole.

Serves 12.

Variation: *Spoon casserole onto plates and pass sour cream and toppings.*

See photograph on page 123.

Enchilada Pie

Any Caballero would love this recipe. This was created by my friend, Deanna, from California, who grew up with Mexican food.

1 lb.	ground beef	500 g
1	medium onion, chopped	1
1	medium green pepper, chopped (optional)	1
28 oz.	can whole tomatoes and juice, chopped	796 mL
2 x 14 oz.	cans tomato sauce	2 x 398 mL
14 oz.	water	398 mL
4 oz.	can green chilies, diced	114 mL
½ cup	sliced black olives	125 mL
1 tsp.	chili powder	5 mL
	salt and pepper to taste	
½ lb.	thinly shredded Cheddar cheese (mild OR sharp, to your taste)	250 g
12	corn tortillas (fresh OR frozen), precooked	12

- Brown meat, onion and green pepper.
- Add roughly chopped tomatoes, tomato sauce and water.
- Add chilies, olives and seasonings.
- Simmer for 20-30 minutes.
- Shred cheese finely and set aside.
- Layer ingredients in a 9 x 13" (23 x 33 cm) pan as follows:
    - 1st layer: sauce
    - 2nd layer: tortillas (tear to fit gaps)
    - 3rd layer: sauce
    - 4th layer: cheese
    - 5th layer: tortillas
    - 6th layer: sauce, then cheese and so on finishing with the cheese.
- Bake in a 350°F (180°C) oven for 30 minutes.

Serves 12.

Note: *This recipe freezes well and may be doubled to feed a large crowd. Serve with a tossed green salad accented with bright red tomatoes. Pass the salsa for those who like things hot.*

Pastitsio

Comfort food from the Greeks.

Really good!!

1½ cups	uncooked macaroni	375 mL
1	egg, beaten	1
⅓ cup	milk	75 mL
½ cup	grated Parmesan cheese	125 mL
1 lb.	lean ground beef	500 g
⅔ cup	chopped onion	150 mL
1 tsp.	cinnamon	5 mL
½ tsp.	pepper	2 mL
7½ oz.	can tomato sauce	213 mL
2 tbsp.	butter OR margarine	30 mL
2 tbsp.	all-purpose flour	30 mL
1 cup	milk	250 mL
¼ cup	beef broth	60 mL
1	egg, lightly beaten	1
¼ cup	grated Parmesan cheese	60 mL
½ cup	grated mozzarella cheese	125 mL

- Boil macaroni until cooked. Drain.
- Add beaten egg, milk and Parmesan cheese. Stir well.
- Pour half of this mixture into a greased 9" (23 cm) square baking pan, saving the other half for the top of casserole.
- In a large skillet, brown ground beef and drain. Add onions and fry until translucent. Add cinnamon, pepper and tomato sauce. Simmer for 5 minutes.
- Spread over macaroni mixture in pan. Spoon remaining macaroni mixture evenly over ground beef mixture.
- In a medium saucepan, melt butter, stir in flour and mix until well combined.
- Add milk, a little at a time, whisking after each addition.
- Add beef broth. Heat until thick and bubbly.
- Add ½ cup (125 mL) of hot mixture to egg while stirring quickly.
- Pour egg mixture back into saucepan. Mix well.
- Add cheeses. Stir until cheese melts.
- Pour sauce over casserole, spreading evenly to edges.
- Bake, uncovered, in 350°F (180°C) oven for 45 minutes.
- Let rest for 5-10 minutes before slicing.
- Serve with a green salad.

Serves 9.

Note: *This is good for company and it can be made ahead.*

Moroccan Meatball Stew

1½ lbs.	lean ground beef	750 g
¼ tsp.	pepper	1 mL
½ tsp.	salt	2 mL
¼ cup	finely chopped onion	60 mL
1	egg	1
¼ cup	milk	60 mL
1 cup	fine bread crumbs	250 mL
28 oz.	can tomatoes, chopped (not drained)	796 mL
10 oz.	can sliced mushrooms (drained)	284 mL
⅓ cup	vinegar	75 mL
⅔ cup	brown sugar	150 mL
2 tsp.	Worcestershire sauce	10 mL
1	green pepper, cut in 1" (2.5 cm) squares	1
2	large carrots, sliced	2
2	celery stalks, in ½" (1.3 cm) slices	2
1	onion, cut in wedges	1
3 tbsp.	cornstarch	45 mL
⅓ cup	cold water	75 mL

- In a large mixing bowl, combine ground beef, pepper, salt, onion salt, egg, milk and bread crumbs.
- Mix well and form into 1½" (4 cm) meatballs.
- Brown meatballs in skillet or in a 400°F (200°C) oven on a baking sheet until meat is no longer pink.
- Drain and place in a large crock pot or 2-quart (2 L) casserole.
- Combine chopped tomatoes, mushrooms, vinegar, brown sugar, Worcestershire sauce and vegetables and pour over meatballs.
- Bake, covered, at 325°F (160°C) for 2 hours (8 hours in a slow cooker).
- Twenty minutes before serving, mix cornstarch with water and quickly stir into sauce mixture.
- Return to oven, covered, for 20 minutes.
- Serve with potatoes or rice.

Serves 8.

Variations: *Substitute stewing beef or beef sausages for meatballs.*

1 large sweet potato peeled and cubed adds interesting flavor to this stew.

Italian Spaghetti Sauce

This is a nice thick sauce with great flavor.

1½ lbs.	lean ground beef	750 mL
1	large onion, diced	1
1	green pepper, diced	1
3	celery stalks, diced	3
2 x 28 oz.	cans tomatoes, diced	2 x 796 mL
3 x 5.5. oz.	cans tomato paste	3 x 156 mL
7½ oz.	can tomato sauce	213 mL
1 tsp.	dried basil leaves	5 mL
1 tsp.	dried thyme leaves	5 mL
1 tsp.	dried oregano leaves	5 mL
2	bay leaves	2
½ tsp.	coarsely ground black pepper	2 mL
½ tsp.	salt	2 mL
1	garlic clove, crushed	1
¾ cup	grated zucchini (optional)	175 mL
½ cup	chopped, pitted black olives (optional)	125 mL
10 oz.	can mushroom pieces and stems, drained (optional)	284 mL

- In a large skillet, brown ground beef and drain.
- Add onion, green pepper and celery. Sauté until onion is translucent then transfer to a 3-4-quart (3-4 L) pot or Dutch oven.
- Add remaining ingredients. Bring to a boil, stirring constantly. Reduce to medium-low heat and simmer, covered, for at least 2 hours.
- Stir occasionally.
- The longer this sauce simmers the more the flavors blend and the better it will taste.

Yield: 20, ½ cup (125 mL) servings.

Variation: *Half the ground beef can be made into small meatballs. Season raw meat with salt and pepper, brown before adding to sauce.*

Lasagne

9	lasagne noodles	9
1½ lbs.	ground beef	750 g
1	medium onion, chopped	1
1	garlic clove, crushed	1
14 oz.	can crushed tomatoes	398 mL
5.5 oz.	can tomato paste	156 mL
⅓ cup	water	75 mL
1 tsp.	dried basil	5 mL
1 tsp.	dried oregano	5 mL
½ tsp.	dried thyme	2 mL
½ tsp.	salt	2 mL
½ tsp.	pepper	2 mL
2 cups	creamed cottage cheese	500 mL
1	egg	1
⅓ cup	grated Parmesan cheese	75 mL
12 oz.	mozzarella cheese, grated (keep 1 cup [250 mL] for filling)	340 g

- Cook noodles according to package direction in boiling, salted and oiled water. Slightly undercook noodles. Drain, rinse and set aside.
- In large skillet, brown ground beef. Drain off fat.
- Add onions and garlic and cook with ground beef until translucent.
- Stir in crushed tomatoes, tomato paste, water, herbs and spices.
- Simmer over medium-low heat for 10 minutes.
- Remove from heat and stir well.
- In a small bowl, combine cottage cheese, egg and Parmesan cheese.
- Grate all the mozzarella cheese. Add 1 cup (250 mL) of grated mozzarella cheese to cottage cheese mixture. Save the rest for the topping.
- Preheat oven to 350°F (180°C).
- In a lightly greased 9 x 13" (23 x 33 cm) pan, place 3 noodles side-by-side lengthwise on bottom.
- Spread ⅓ of meat mixture over noodles and cover with 3 more noodles.
- Spread cottage cheese mixture over noodles; spread ⅓ more meat mixture over cottage cheese then add another layer of noodles.
- Spread remaining meat mixture over noodles.
- Sprinkle remaining mozzarella cheese evenly over top. Bake for 35-40 minutes. Let sit for 10 minutes before cutting.
- Serve with Caesar Salad, page 75, and Herb and Garlic Bread, page 40.

Serves 12.

Souper Macaroni Casserole

This is a tasty quick fix for busy nights. It is easy for kids to prepare.

1½ cups	uncooked elbow macaroni	375 mL
1 lb.	ground beef	500 g
½ cup	chopped onion	125 mL
¼ tsp.	salt	1 mL
¼ tsp.	pepper	1 mL
10 oz.	can mushroom soup, undiluted	284 mL
10 oz.	can tomato soup, undiluted	284 mL
19 oz.	can tomatoes, drained and chopped	540 mL
	grated mild, medium OR sharp Cheddar cheese	

- Cook macaroni in boiling water with 1 tsp. (5 mL) of oil until done. Check package for timing. Drain.
- While macaroni is cooking, brown ground beef in a large skillet and drain off fat.
- Add onion, salt and pepper. Sauté until onion is translucent.
- Stir in mushroom and tomato soups and the tomatoes.
- Stir in the cooked macaroni.
- Heat thoroughly.
- Serve with cheese sprinkled on top and a tossed salad on the side.

Serves 6.

Variation: *For a Cheeseburger Casserole, stir 1 cup (250 mL) of grated Cheddar cheese into casserole after macaroni is added.*

Cheesy-Rice Meat Roll

Even those who don't like meat loaf will love this one.

1½ lbs.	lean ground beef	750 g
½ cup	cracker OR bread crumbs	125 mL
1	egg	1
¼ cup	milk OR water	60 mL
½ tsp.	Worcestershire sauce	2 mL
1 tsp.	instant beef bouillon granules	5 mL
1 tsp.	salt	5 mL
¼ tsp.	pepper	1 mL
½ cup	finely chopped onion	125 mL
1 tsp.	onion powder	5 mL
½ cup	ketchup	125 mL
¼ cup	brown sugar	60 mL
1 tbsp.	prepared mustard	15 mL
1½ cups	cooked rice	375 mL
1 cup	shredded cheese (any kind of hard cheese)	250 mL
1 tsp.	oregano	5 mL
¼ tsp.	salt	1 mL
¼ tsp.	pepper	1 mL

- Mix first 10 ingredients together and let sit for 10 minutes.
- Roll out meat mixture between 2 sheets of waxed paper to a 10 x 13" (25 x 33 cm) rectangle.
- Remove top piece of paper. Combine ketchup, brown sugar and mustard. Spread half of this mixture over meat.
- In a small bowl, mix together rice, cheese, oregano, salt and pepper.
- Sprinkle evenly over meat.
- Beginning on the 10" (25 cm) side, carefully roll up meat and rice mixture like a jelly roll, using waxed paper underneath to start roll.
- DO NOT ROLL UP WAXED PAPER WITH MEAT.
- Press together the seam at the end. Seal the sides.
- Carefully transfer roll to a 9 x 13" (23 x 33 cm) pan, seam side down.
- Spread remaining half of sauce evenly over the roll.
- Bake at 350°F (180°C) for 60-70 minutes.
- Let sit for 10 minutes before slicing.

Serves 6-8.

Beef

Make-Ahead Enchilada Casserole, page 115

Cornish Pasties

These flavorful little meat pies originated in Cornwall, England as a self-contained lunch for the tin miners. Often a meat and vegetable mixture was put on one side and a fruit mixture on the other side, a complete meal in one pastry.

1 lb.	lean ground beef OR diced cooked beef	500 g
½ cup	finely chopped onion	125 mL
1	celery stalk, thinly sliced	1
2	medium carrots, peeled and grated	2
1	large potato, peeled and grated	1
¼ cup	peas (optional)	60 mL
10 oz.	can mushroom soup (undiluted)	284 mL
2½ tsp.	soy sauce	12 mL
1 tbsp.	Worcestershire sauce	15 mL
	salt and pepper to taste	
	pie pastry, page 174	

- In a large skillet, fry ground beef until brown. Omit this step for cooked beef.
- To skillet, add onions and celery. Fry until tender-crisp. If using cooked beef, sauté onions and celery in 1 tbsp. (15 mL) oil.
- Add remaining ingredients and stir until well mixed.
- Cover skillet and simmer over medium-low heat until vegetables are cooked, stirring occasionally. Cool and set aside.
- Prepare pastry. Roll out pastry thinly. Place a cereal bowl, bottom up, on pastry and cut around it with a knife. Make several rounds.
- Place 2 heaping spoonfuls of ground beef mixture in the center of each circle. Spread evenly over ½ the circle but leave ½" (1.3 cm) around the edges.
- Fold over circle and pinch pastry together, with a fork, around the open edges.
- Cut 3 slits in the top.
- Continue doing this until ground beef mixture or pastry is used up.
- Transfer pasties to a baking sheet and bake at 375°F (190°C) until pastry is golden brown, about 20 minutes.

Yield: 1 dozen pasties.

Note: *These freeze well. Freeze on baking sheets before baking. Transfer to freezer bags when frozen. To bake, place frozen pasties on a baking sheet and bake the same as for fresh but 5 minutes longer. Do not thaw before baking.*

Variation: *Use a 3" (7 cm) round cookie cutter and make appetizer-sized Cornish Pasties.*

See photograph on the front cover.

Meat-Filled Buns

Great for camping trips or lunch boxes as they're good hot or cold.

1	recipe bun OR bread dough, page 33, OR frozen bread dough	1
2 lbs.	lean ground beef	1 kg
1 cup	diced onion	250 mL
½ tsp.	salt	2 mL
½ tsp.	pepper	2 mL
2 tsp.	instant beef granules (optional)	10 mL
2 cups	grated Cheddar cheese	500 mL
⅔ cup	ketchup OR barbecue sauce OR spaghetti sauce	150 mL

- Prepare bread dough and put to rise.
- While dough is rising, prepare filling.
- In a large skillet, brown ground beef and drain.
- Add onion and fry until onion is translucent.
- Remove from heat, stir in the remaining ingredients and set aside.
- When dough has risen the amount of times necessary in the dough recipe, punch down and divide into 24 pieces.
- Form each piece into a ball and flatten.
- Place a heaping tablespoon (30 mL) of the meat mixture in the center of the dough.
- Bring the dough up from the sides and pinch the ends together to seal in the meat. Press down lightly to evenly distribute filling inside bun.
- Place on a greased baking sheet, seam side down.
- Let rise in a warm place until double (45 minutes).
- Bake at 350°F (180°C) for 20 minutes.

Yield: 24 meat buns.

Variation:

Pizza-Filled Buns: Use chopped ham or pepperoni or ground beef, pizza sauce, chopped green pepper and mozzarella cheese as a filling.

Note: *These freeze well. Put in bags in freezer when cool. To serve, pop in microwave on defrost for 5 minutes or warm in oven at 300°F (150°C) for 20 minutes.*

Desserts
&
Sweets

Grandma's Ginger Cookies

Excellent for Gingerbread Men and Crackle Top Cookies. My Grandmother's original recipe called for lard but I have adapted it to modern times by using butter or margarine for a better flavor.

½ cup	butter or margarine	125 mL
½ cup	fancy molasses	125 mL
½ cup	brown sugar	125 mL
1	egg	1
2 cups	flour	500 mL
1 tsp.	baking soda	5 mL
1 tsp.	cinnamon	5 mL
1 tsp.	ginger	5 mL
1 tsp.	mace	5 mL
¼ tsp.	cloves (optional)	1 mL

- In a large mixing bowl, cream butter, molasses and brown sugar until well mixed.
- Add egg and beat until light and fluffy.
- Combine flour, baking soda and spices.
- Stir into egg mixture, a little at a time, until well mixed.
- Wrap in plastic and refrigerate for 1 hour to let spices blend.
- Preheat oven to 350°F (180°C).
- Roll out dough thinly and cut into shapes.
- Place on lightly greased cookie sheets and bake for 5-8 minutes.
- Remove to cooling racks.
- Decorate with your favorite frosting.

Yield: 2½ dozen cookies.

Note: *This recipe makes great gingerbread houses. Bake in flat sheets and cut into desired shapes. Use Royal Icing, page 154, to glue pieces together.*

Variation:

Crackle Top Ginger Cookies: *Roll dough in 1½" (4 cm) balls and dip in granulated sugar. Place 2" (5 cm) apart on cookie sheet. Flatten slightly. Bake at 350°F (180°C) for 10-12 minutes.*

See photograph on page 175.

Grandma's Sugar Cookies

Great for Valentine cookies.

½ cup	butter OR margarine	125 mL
½ cup	brown sugar	125 mL
1	egg	1
1½ cups	flour	375 mL
1½ tsp.	baking powder	7 mL
¼ cup	milk	60 mL

- In a large mixing bowl, cream butter and sugar together.
- Add egg and beat until light and fluffy.
- Mix flour and baking powder together.
- Add to butter mixture alternately with milk until well mixed.
- Chill dough.
- Preheat oven to 350°F (180°C).
- Roll out dough thinly on a lightly floured surface and cut out shapes with cookie cutters.
- Place on a lightly greased cookie sheet.
- Bake for 5-8 minutes.
- Sprinkle with sugar halfway through baking, if desired.
- Remove from oven.
- If cookies are not sprinkled with sugar, spread with your favorite frosting. Try pink for Valentine cookies.

Yield: 2 dozen cookies.

Variation:
Filled Cookies: *Spread date filling, page 141, between 2 cookies.*

Hint: *Bake cookies on a rack in the centre of the oven to prevent burning the bottoms. If you use cookie sheets without edges, rather than baking pans with edges, the cookies will bake more evenly because the hot air circulates over them more evenly.*

Butter Crisps

Great for cutout cookies at Christmas.

1 cup	butter OR margarine	250 mL
5 tbsp.	icing sugar	75 mL
½ tsp.	almond extract OR vanilla	2 mL
2 cups	sifted flour	500 mL
2 tbsp.	cornstarch	30 mL

- Beat butter until light and fluffy.
- Add icing sugar and almond extract and continue beating.
- Sift flour and cornstarch together and beat into butter mixture a little at a time.
- Preheat oven to 325°F (160°C).
- Roll out dough on a lightly floured counter and cut into desired shapes.
- Place on an ungreased cookie sheet.
- Top with a cherry or an almond, if desired.
- Bake for about 12 minutes, or until bottoms and edges are very light brown.
- Cool on a rack.
- Cookies may be frosted with a Butter-Cream Icing, page 155, or drizzled with melted chocolate or dip cookie tops right in melted chocolate. Sprinkle with finely ground almonds.

Yield: 4 dozen cookies.

Nutty Sugar and Spice Shortbread

This delicate cookie will literally melt in your mouth.

1 cup	butter (do not use margarine)	250 mL
⅓ cup	sugar	75 mL
1 tsp.	vanilla	5 mL
1¾ cups	flour	425 mL
½ cup	finely ground walnuts OR pecans	125 mL
⅓ cup	sugar	75 mL
1 tbsp.	cinnamon	15 mL

Nutty Sugar and Spice Shortbread
Continued

- In a large bowl, beat butter for 5 minutes until light and fluffy.
- Add ⅓ cup (75 mL) sugar and vanilla and beat well.
- Beat in flour and nuts.
- Preheat oven to 325°F (160°C).
- This is a very delicate dough — so roll out lightly on a floured surface.
- Cut into shapes (stars, crescents, rounds) and place on an ungreased cookie sheet.
- Bake in the centre of the oven for 15 minutes, or until lightly browned on sides and bottoms.
- Mix ⅓ cup (75 mL) sugar and cinnamon together in a bowl.
- Remove cookies from the oven and coat with sugar, cinnamon mixture while still warm.

Yield: 2 dozen cookies.

Whipped Shortbread
These shortbread cookies are very light.

2 cups	butter (do not use margarine)	500 mL
1 cup	icing sugar	250 mL
3 cups	flour	750 mL

- In a large mixing bowl, beat butter for 5 minutes with electric mixer.
- Add icing sugar and beat another 2 minutes. Add flour, ½ cup (125 mL) at a time, beating and scraping sides of bowl after each addition.
- Preheat oven to 325°F (160°C).
- Drop dough by heaping teaspoonfuls (7 mL) or press through a cookie press onto ungreased cookie sheets.
- Garnish with glacé or maraschino cherry halves, pecan or almond halves.
- Bake for 10-15 minutes, or until very light brown.
- After cookies are cooled, you can dip half of each cookie in melted chocolate.

Yield: 3 dozen cookies.

Variation: *For Rolled Shortbread Cookies, add 1 cup (250 mL) more flour. Roll out on a floured surface and cut with your favorite cookie cutters. Reduce heat to 300°F (150°C) bake for 10-15 minutes, or until very light golden brown on the bottom.*

131

Peanut Butter Oatmeal Cookies

This chewy oatmeal cookie has a peanut butter flavor.

1 cup	butter OR margarine	250 mL
¾ cup	brown sugar	175 mL
¾ cup	white sugar	175 mL
½ cup	peanut butter, chunky OR smooth	125 mL
1	egg	1
1 tsp.	vanilla	5 mL
½ tsp.	salt	2 mL
1½ cups	flour	375 mL
1 tsp.	baking soda	5 mL
1¼ cups	rolled oats	300 mL

- In a large mixing bowl, beat butter, sugars and peanut butter until well creamed.
- Add egg, vanilla and salt. Beat until fluffy.
- In a separate bowl, combine flour and baking soda.
- Add to creamed mixture and beat until well blended.
- Stir in oats.
- Preheat oven to 350°F (180°C).
- Roll dough into 1" (2.5 cm) balls and place 2" (5 cm) apart on ungreased cookie sheets.
- Slightly flatten with the bottom of a glass dipped in sugar.
- Bake for 10-12 minutes, or until lightly browned.

Yield: 4 dozen cookies.

Variation: *For Peanut Butter Chocolate Chip Oatmeal Cookies add 1 cup (250 mL) chocolate chips to this recipe.*

See photograph on page 175.

Big Batch Oatmeal Cookies

Soft and chewy.

1½ cups	butter OR margarine	375 mL
1½ cups	white sugar	375 mL
1½ cups	brown sugar	375 mL
3	eggs	3
2 tsp.	vanilla	10 mL
¼ cup	milk	60 mL
3 cups	flour	750 mL
1½ tsp.	baking soda	7 mL
1 tbsp.	baking powder	15 mL
½ tsp.	salt	2 mL
3 cups	rolled oats	750 mL
¾ cup	coconut	175 mL
3 cups	chocolate chips OR raisins OR both	750 mL
1½ cups	crushed cornflakes (optional)	375 mL

- In a large bowl, cream butter and sugars.
- Add eggs, vanilla and milk. Beat until light and fluffy.
- Combine flour, baking soda, baking powder and salt.
- Add to creamed mixture 1 cup (250 mL) at a time.
- Mix until well-blended.
- Sir in rolled oats, coconut, chocolate chips or raisins and cornflakes, if using.
- Preheat oven to 350°F (180°C).
- Drop dough by heaping teaspoonfuls (10 mL) onto an ungreased baking sheet.
- Bake for 10-12 minutes.

Yield: 7 dozen cookies.

Variation: *Glacé cherries or mixed dry fruit are also good additions to these cookies.*

Hint: *A 1½" (4 cm) diameter ice-cream scoop is ideal for dropping cookie dough onto baking sheets.*

Crispy Date and Cherry Balls

My Aunt Mary from California got me hooked on these.
They are an attractive addition to Christmas cookie trays.

¼ cup	butter	60 mL
1 cup	sugar	250 mL
1½ cups	chopped dates	375 mL
2 tbsp.	water	30 mL
1½ cups	coconut (medium flake)	375 mL
1½ cups	Rice Krispies	375 mL
½ cup	finely chopped walnuts OR pecans	125 mL
⅓ cup	chopped maraschino cherries	75 mL
	coconut for rolling	

- In a large saucepan, melt butter; add sugar, dates and water.
- Stir over medium heat to melt everything into a paste-like consistency.
- Remove from heat, cool slightly, and add remaining ingredients.
- Form into 1" (2.5 cm) balls.
- Roll in coconut.
- These freeze well.

Yield: 3 dozen cookies.

Chocolate Chip Cookies

Excellent flavor and texture — a soft cookie.

1 cup	butter OR margarine	250 mL
⅔ cup	brown sugar	150 mL
½ cup	white sugar	125 mL
⅓ cup	honey (warmed until runny)	75 mL
2	eggs	2
1 tsp.	vanilla	5 mL
½ tsp.	salt	2 mL
3½ cups	all-purpose flour	875 mL
1 tsp.	baking soda	5 mL
1 cup	chocolate chips	250 mL

Chocolate Chip Cookies

Continued

- In a large mixing bowl, cream butter, sugars and honey.
- Add eggs, vanilla and salt, beating until light and fluffy.
- Combine flour and baking soda. Slowly add to creamed mixture, beating until well blended. Stir in chocolate chips.
- Roll dough in 1½" (4 cm) balls and place 2" (5 cm) apart on an ungreased cookie sheet. Flatten with bottom of a glass dipped in flour to prevent sticking.
- Bake at 350°F (180°C) for 8-10 minutes.

Yield: 4 dozen cookies.

Hint: *Watch closely because the honey makes the cookies brown quickly.*

Deep Chocolate-Chocolate Chip Cookies

For those who really like chocolate.

½ cup	shortening	125 mL
¾ cup	butter OR margarine	175 mL
1½ cups	sugar	375 mL
2	eggs	2
2⅓ cups	flour	575 mL
¾ cup	cocoa	175 mL
2 tsp.	baking soda	10 mL
1 cup	chocolate chips	250 mL
½ cup	chopped walnuts OR pecans	125 mL

- In a large mixing bowl, cream together shortening and butter.
- Beat in sugar and eggs until light and fluffy.
- Mix flour, cocoa and baking soda together.
- Beat dry ingredients into egg mixture. Stir until well mixed.
- Stir in chocolate chips and nuts.
- Form dough into 1½" (4 cm) balls and place on an ungreased cookie sheet.
- Bake at 350°F (180°C) for 8-10 minutes.

Yield: 2½ dozen cookies.

Variations: *Add Smarties or Reeses Pieces instead of chocolate chips. Cookie dough may be dropped by spoonfuls onto baking sheets instead of forming it into balls.*

See photograph on page 175.

Whoopie Pies (Soft Oreo Cookies)

"Whoopie I Ki Yay" — They'll be galloping all the way home for one of these treats. Make these for the next school party.

1 cup	shortening	250 mL
2 cups	sugar	500 mL
2	eggs	2
1 cup	sour milk	250 mL
1 tsp.	vanilla	5 mL
4 cups	flour	1 L
1 cup	cocoa	250 mL
1 tsp.	salt	5 mL
1 cup	hot water	250 mL
2 tsp.	baking soda	10 mL

- Preheat oven to 375°F (190°C).
- In a large mixing bowl, cream shortening and sugar. Add eggs and beat well.
- Combine milk and vanilla.
- Sift together flour, cocoa and salt. Add to creamed mixture alternately with milk. Add water (reserve ¼ cup [60 mL]) and mix until smooth.
- To ¼ cup (60 mL) water, add baking soda. Stir this mixture into batter.
- Drop the thick batter onto a greased cookie sheet with a spoon.
- Bake for 8 minutes. Watch carefully as you don't want them to burn, but they need to be completely baked. They should look dry, not wet. Cool the cookies thoroughly.
- To fill, spread a fairly generous amount of filling (see below) on the flat side of the cookie and top with another cookie.

Yield: 4 dozen cookies.

Hint: *One trick I use is to wet a spoon and smooth the mound of batter slightly, making more uniform and somewhat flatter cookies. Do not flatten with the spoon, just smooth the top.*

Creamy Filling

2	egg whites	2
2 tsp.	vanilla	10 mL
4 tsp.	milk	20 mL
4 tsp.	flour	20 mL
4 cups	icing sugar	1 L
½ cup	shortening	125 mL

- Cream first 4 ingredients with 2 cups (500 mL) of icing sugar; add remaining icing sugar plus shortening. The shortening makes the filling really white.

Nanaimo Bars

Everybody's favorite with delicious variations.

Base:
½ cup	butter OR margarine	125 mL
¼ cup	sugar	60 mL
¼ cup	cocoa	60 mL
1	egg, beaten	1
1 tsp.	vanilla	5 mL
1⅔ cups	graham wafer crumbs	400 mL
1 cup	fine coconut	250 mL
⅔ cup	finely chopped walnuts	150 mL

Filling:
¼ cup	butter	60 mL
2 cups	icing sugar	500 mL
2 tbsp.	custard powder	30 mL
2 tbsp.	milk	30 mL
½ tsp.	vanilla	2 mL

Topping:
3 x 1 oz.	squares semisweet chocolate	3 x 30 g
1 tbsp.	butter OR margarine	30 mL

- To make the base, heat the butter, sugar and cocoa in the double boiler; stir until smooth. Add egg and vanilla and stir until well blended. Remove from heat and add crumbs, coconut and walnuts. Stir well. Press evenly into a greased 9" (23 cm) square pan. Refrigerate.
- To prepare the filling, beat butter, icing sugar and custard powder together. Beat in milk and vanilla until smooth. Spread evenly over cooled base. Refrigerate until firm.
- To prepare topping, melt chocolate and butter in a double boiler and mix well. Spread over cooled filling and refrigerate until chocolate is set. Slice and serve.

Yield: 25 bars.

Variations:

Cherry Almond Nanaimo Bars: *Base — substitute almonds for walnuts. Filling — substitute 2 tbsp. (30 mL) maraschino cherry juice for milk and add ¼ cup (60 mL) chopped red maraschino cherries. Substitute ½ tsp. (2 mL) almond extract for vanilla.*

Minty Nanaimo Bars: *Filling — substitute 1 tsp. (5 mL) peppermint extract for vanilla. Tint with green food coloring.*

Peanut Butter Nanaimo Bars: *Base — substitute peanuts for walnuts. Filling — add ¼ cup (60 mL) peanut butter and increase milk to 3 tbsp. (45 mL).*

Caramel Nougat Squares

These taste similar to Mars Bars.

First Layer:

¼ cup	butter OR margarine	60 mL
¼ cup	sugar	60 mL
2 tbsp.	cocoa	30 mL
1	egg, beaten	1
1 cup	fine coconut	250 mL
2 cups	Oreo OR chocolate wafer crumbs	500 mL
½ cup	finely chopped almonds	125 mL

Second Layer:

1	egg white	1
2 tbsp.	corn syrup	30 mL
½ cup	sugar	125 mL
½ cup	corn syrup	125 mL
1 tbsp. + 2 tsp.	water	25 mL
½ tsp.	vanilla OR almond extract	2 mL
½ cup	chopped slivered almonds	125 mL

Third Layer:

½ cup	butter OR margarine	125 mL
½ cup	brown sugar	125 mL
2 tbsp.	corn syrup	30 mL
⅔ cup	sweetened condensed milk, page 200	150 mL

Topping:

1 cup	chocolate chips	250 mL

- To prepare the first layer, in a medium saucepan, melt butter and sugar together until sugar is dissolved. Remove from heat. Beat in cocoa and beaten egg. Stir in coconut, Oreo crumbs and nuts. Press into a 9" (23 cm) square pan. Cool.
- To prepare the second layer, in a small mixing bowl, beat egg white plus 2 tbsp. (30 mL) corn syrup until stiff peaks form. In a small saucepan, heat sugar, corn syrup and water to a full rolling boil. Boil at a rolling boil until temperature reaches 275°F (140°C) and remove from heat. Pour hot mixture over egg white mixture while beating with an electric mixer. Beat until well blended and very thick. Quickly beat in vanilla. Stir in almonds. Spread over first layer and refrigerate.

Caramel Nougat Squares
Continued

- To prepare the third layer, in a small saucepan, melt butter, brown sugar, corn syrup and sweetened condensed milk over medium heat, stirring constantly. Bring to a boil and boil for 5 minutes continuing to stir constantly. Remove from heat and beat with a wooden spoon for about 30 seconds. Pour over the nougat mixture and return to the refrigerator to cool.
- To prepare the topping over hot water in a double boiler, melt chocolate chips. Spread over caramel layer. Cool and slice.

Yield: 25 bars.

Granola Bars
These are better than the ones you buy.

1	recipe granola, page 190	1
2 cups	Rice Krispies	500 mL
1/2 cup	butter OR margarine	125 mL
1/3 cup	honey OR corn syrup	75 mL
14 oz.	pkg. marshmallows	400 g
1 cup	peanut butter	250 mL

- In a large bowl, mix granola and Rice Krispies.
- In a large pot, heat butter and honey over medium heat until melted.
- Add marshmallows and stir until melted.
- Add peanut butter and stir until well blended, then remove from heat.
- Pour butter mixture over granola mixture and mix thoroughly.
- Press into a greased 10 x 15" (25 x 38 cm) pan.
- Refrigerate for 30 minutes then slice into squares.
- These freeze well.

Yield: 40 bars.

Variation: *Cool slightly then press 1/2-3/4 cup (125-175 mL) of chocolate chips into the flattened mixture in the pan. If they are added when the mixture is hot, they will melt.*

Lemon Crumble Bars

Base:

1 cup	flour	250 mL
¼ cup	icing sugar	60 mL
½ cup	butter OR margarine	125 mL

Filling:

¾ cup	cold water	175 mL
¼ cup	lemon juice	60 mL
⅔ cup	sugar	150 mL
2 tbsp.	cornstarch	30 mL
1	egg, beaten	1
½ tsp.	grated lemon rind	2 mL
1 tbsp.	butter OR margarine	15 mL

Topping:

¼ cup	sugar	60 mL
½ cup	long-thread coconut	125 mL
½ cup	flour	125 mL
½ cup	soda cracker crumbs	125 mL
⅓ cup	butter OR margarine	75 mL

- Preheat oven to 350°F (180°C).
- In a medium mixing bowl, mix flour, icing sugar and butter together until mixture is crumbly and resembles coarse meal.
- Press into the bottom of a 9" (23 cm) square pan.
- Bake at 350°F (180°C) for 10 minutes.
- In a small saucepan, combine cold water, lemon juice, sugar and cornstarch. Cook over medium-low heat until thick and clear.
- Add a small amount of hot mixture to egg and mix well, then pour back into hot mixture and cook for 1 more minute.
- Stir in lemon rind and butter.
- Pour over baked base.
- Mix sugar, coconut, flour, cracker crumbs and butter together until crumbly.
- Sprinkle over lemon filling and bake for 20-30 minutes, or until golden brown.

Yield: 25 squares.

Date Squares (Matrimonial Cake)

This is always a favorite at wedding receptions.

1 cup	flour	250 mL
1 cup	rolled oats	250 mL
¼ tsp.	salt	1 mL
½ tsp.	baking soda	2 mL
½ cup	brown sugar	125 mL
½ cup	butter OR margarine	125 mL
1	egg yolk	1
1 cup	chopped dates	250 mL
½ cup	hot water	125 mL
2 tbsp.	sugar	30 mL
1 tsp.	vanilla	5 mL

- In a large mixing bowl, combine flour, oats, salt, baking soda and brown sugar.
- Add butter and cut in or rub in until mixture resembles coarse meal.
- Divide mixture into 2 equal parts.
- Add the egg yolk to 1 of the equal parts of crumb mixture and stir until evenly mixed.
- Press egg-crumb mixture into a greased 9" (23 cm) square pan and set aside.
- To prepare date filling, in a saucepan, combine dates, water, sugar and vanilla. Cook over medium heat until dates are soft and smooth, like jam.
- Cool and spread over base.
- Preheat oven to 350°F (180°C).
- Sprinkle remaining crumb mixture evenly over dates, press lightly.
- Bake for 25-30 minutes, or until golden brown.
- Cool and slice.

Yield: 25 squares.

Variation:

Blueberry Squares: — *replace date filling with blueberry filling:*

2 cups	blueberries	500 mL
⅔ cup	sugar	150 mL
3 tbsp.	cornstarch	45 mL
¼ cup	water	60 mL

- In a medium-sized saucepan, heat blueberries and sugar together until sugar dissolves. Mix cornstarch and cold water together. Pour into hot mixture and cook until thick. Prepare and assemble the squares as above.

Butter Tart Bars

These taste like Butter Tarts, but are much easier to make.

1 cup	flour	250 mL
2 tbsp.	icing sugar	30 mL
2 tbsp.	brown sugar	30 mL
½ cup	butter OR margarine	125 mL
2	eggs	2
1 cup	brown sugar	250 mL
2 tbsp.	flour	30 mL
½ tsp.	baking powder	2 mL
½ tsp.	vanilla	2 mL
⅛ tsp.	salt	0.5 mL
2 tbsp.	corn syrup	30 mL
2 tbsp.	melted butter	30 mL
⅔ cup	raisins	150 mL
½ cup	chopped walnuts OR pecans	125 mL

- Preheat oven to 350°F (180°C).
- In a medium-sized mixing bowl, combine flour, icing sugar and 2 tbsp. (30 mL) brown sugar.
- Add butter and cut in until mixture resembles coarse meal.
- Press into a 9" (23 cm) square baking pan.
- Bake for 10 minutes. Remove from oven.
- In a medium-sized mixing bowl, combine eggs, 1 cup (250 mL) brown sugar, flour, baking powder, vanilla, salt, corn syrup and melted butter. Beat until syrupy.
- Stir in raisins and nuts and pour over base.
- Bake for another 20-25 minutes, or until just about firm.
- Cool and cut into 36 small squares.

Yield: 36 small squares.

Chocolate Brownies

Moist and chewy, the way Brownies should be.

½ cup	butter OR margarine, melted	125 mL
½ cup	brown sugar	125 mL
½ cup	white sugar	125 mL
2	eggs	2
⅓ cup	cocoa	75 mL
½ tsp.	salt	2 mL
1 tsp.	vanilla	5 mL
¾ cup	flour	175 mL
½ cup	chopped walnuts OR pecans	125 mL
	Chocolate Buttercream Frosting, page 154	
	chopped nuts for topping	

- Preheat oven to 350°F (180°C).
- In a medium-sized bowl, mix together butter, sugars, eggs, cocoa, salt and vanilla and beat well.
- Stir in flour and nuts.
- Pour into a greased 9" (23 cm) square pan.
- Bake for 25 minutes.
- When cool spread with Chocolate Buttercream Frosting.
- Sprinkle with chopped nuts.

Yield: 25 brownies.

Variation:
Cherry Brownies: *Substitute ⅓ cup (75 mL) chopped maraschino cherries for nuts.*

Chocolate Carrot Snack Cake

Supermoist and delicious.

½ cup	oil	60 mL
¾ cup	sugar	175 mL
1	egg	1
½ tsp.	vanilla	2 mL
1 cup	grated carrots	250 mL
1 cup	flour	250 mL
3 tbsp.	cocoa	45 mL
½ tsp.	baking powder	2 mL
½ tsp.	cinnamon	2 mL
½ tsp.	baking soda	2 mL
¼ tsp.	allspice OR cloves	1 mL
½ cup	buttermilk OR sour milk	125 mL
½ cup	walnuts	125 mL

- Preheat oven to 350°F (180°C).
- In a medium-sized mixing bowl, combine oil, sugar, egg and vanilla. Beat until smooth.
- Stir in carrots.
- Combine all dry ingredients and spices.
- Add alternately with buttermilk, beating well after each addition.
- Stir in walnuts.
- Pour into a greased 9" (23 cm) square pan.
- Bake for 30-35 minutes, or until a toothpick inserted in center comes out clean.
- Let cool and frost with Cream Cheese Frosting, page 155, or Chocolate Buttercream Frosting, page 154, or leave plain.

Yield: 9" (23 cm) square pan.

Moist and Spicy Carrot Cake

This carrot cake is true to its name.

½ cup	oil	125 mL
1 cup	sugar	250 mL
2	eggs	2
1½ cups	grated carrots	375 mL
1 cup	flour	250 mL
½ tsp.	salt	2 mL
1 tsp.	baking soda	5 mL
1 tsp.	cinnamon	5 mL
¼ tsp.	mace	1 mL
¼ tsp.	allspice	1 mL
¼ cup	shredded coconut	60 mL
⅓ cup	chopped raisins	75 mL
¼ cup	chopped pecans OR walnuts	60 mL

- Preheat oven to 350°F (180°C).
- In a medium-sized mixing bowl, combine oil, sugar and eggs and beat until light and fluffy.
- Add carrots.
- Sift dry ingredients together and add coconut, raisins and nuts. Stir to mix.
- Stir flour and nut mixture into sugar and egg mixture and mix until well moistened.
- Pour batter into a 9" (23 cm) square pan.
- Bake for 25-30 minutes, or until a toothpick inserted in the center comes out clean.
- Frost with Cream Cheese Frosting, page 155, and sprinkle top with chopped walnuts or pecans.

Yield: 9" (23 cm) square cake.

Carrot Cake Roll

A novel way to prepare the ever-popular carrot cake.

3	eggs	3
1 cup	sugar	250 mL
3/4 cup	finely grated carrots	175 mL
1 tsp.	vanilla	5 mL
1 cup	all-purpose flour	250 mL
1 tsp.	baking powder	5 mL
1 1/2 tsp.	cinnamon	7 mL
1/4 tsp.	mace	1 mL
3/4 cup	chopped walnuts	175 mL
	icing sugar	
	Mock Cream Cheese Frosting, page 153	

- Preheat oven to 350°F (180°C).
- Grease and flour a 10 x 15" (25 x 38 cm) jelly roll pan or baking pan. Line the bottom with waxed paper.
- In a mixing bowl, beat eggs for 4 minutes on high speed.
- Slowly add sugar to eggs while beating and beat for 2 more minutes.
- Stir in carrots and vanilla and set bowl aside.
- In another bowl, mix flour, baking powder, cinnamon and mace.
- Fold flour mixture into egg mixture, until evenly blended. Pour into pan spreading batter evenly. Sprinkle nuts over batter. DO NOT MIX INTO BATTER.
- Bake for 12-15 minutes, or until a toothpick comes out clean.
- Remove cake from oven and invert onto a tea towel sprinkled with icing sugar. Nut side should be touching icing sugar. Remove waxed paper.
- Immediately roll up cake and towel together with nuts on outside of roll. Cool on a cooling rack.
- When cool, gently unroll and spread with Mock Cream Cheese Frosting.
- Reroll cake without towel and place on a serving dish.
- Refrigerate for 3 hours then slice to serve.

Yield: 13, 3/4" (3 cm) slices.

Variation: *If you do not have a fine grater, cook and mash carrots until smooth. Add 3/4 cup (175 mL) carrot purée instead of grated carrots. Carrot baby food also works well. This variation will make a more moist roll. It freezes very well.*

See photograph on page 175.

Moist Dark Apple Cake

This cake takes on different colors depending on which type of apple is used.

2 cups	sugar	500 mL
2	eggs	2
½ cup	oil	125 mL
2 tsp.	vanilla	10 mL
4 cups	peeled, diced OR grated apples (food processor may be used)	1 L
2 cups	flour	500 mL
½ tsp.	nutmeg	2 mL
2 tsp.	cinnamon	10 mL
2 tsp.	baking soda	10 mL
¼ tsp.	salt	1 mL
½ cup	chopped walnuts	125 mL

- Preheat oven to 350°F (180°C).
- In a large mixing bowl, combine sugar, eggs, oil and vanilla until well blended.
- Stir in apples until well mixed.
- Sift together dry ingredients.
- Stir dry mixture into apple mixture mixing well.
- Pour batter into a greased and floured 9 x 13" (23 x 33 cm) pan.
- Bake for 35-40 minutes, or until a toothpick comes out clean.
- Frost with Cream Cheese Frosting, page 155, or Cooked Frosting, page 153.
- This cake can be frosted and served in the pan or it may be cut into squares and placed on a platter to serve.

Yield: 9 x 13" (23 x 33 cm) square cake.

Grandma's Banana Loaf

This is an old standby for bake sales.

½ cup	butter OR margarine, melted	125 mL
1 cup	puréed bananas (3 medium)	250 mL
½ cup	sour cream	125 mL
2 tsp.	vanilla	10 mL
1	egg	1
2 cups	flour	500 mL
1 tsp.	baking soda	5 mL
½ tsp.	salt	2 mL
½ tsp.	cinnamon	2 mL
½ tsp.	ginger	2 mL
¼ tsp.	nutmeg	1 mL
1 cup	sugar	250 mL
¾ cup	chopped walnuts	175 mL

- Preheat oven to 350°F (180°C).
- In a small mixing bowl, combine butter, puréed bananas, sour cream, vanilla and egg. Beat until smooth and set aside.
- In a large mixing bowl, combine remaining ingredients including nuts. Stir to mix all dry ingredients. Make a well in the dry ingredients.
- Add wet ingredients and stir until moistened.
- Pour into a greased and floured loaf pan.
- Bake for 50-60 minutes, or until a toothpick inserted in the middle comes out clean.
- This freezes well.

Yield: 1 loaf or 1 dozen muffins.

Variation:

Banana Chocolate Chip Muffins: *Add ½ cup (125 mL) chocolate chips to the Banana Loaf batter.*

Banana Layer Cake

2 ¼ cups	flour	550 mL
½ tsp.	baking powder	2 mL
1 tsp.	baking soda	5 mL
½ tsp.	salt	2 mL
1 ¼ cups	sugar	300 mL
½ cup	butter OR margarine	125 mL
2	eggs	2
1 cup	puréed bananas	250 mL
½ tsp.	vanilla	2 mL
⅓ cup	sour milk	75 mL

- Preheat oven to 350°F (180°C).
- Sift flour, baking powder, baking soda and salt together twice and set aside.
- In a large mixing bowl, beat together sugar and butter until light and fluffy.
- Add eggs, bananas and vanilla and beat until thoroughly mixed.
- Add sour milk, alternately with sifted dry ingredients, beating until smooth after each addition.
- Pour into 2 greased 9" (23 cm) pans or 1, 9 x 13" (23 x 33 cm) pan.
- Bake for approximately 30 minutes, or until a toothpick comes out clean.
- Fill and frost with Cooked Frosting, page 153.

Yield: 9" (23 cm) layer cake.

*Some cause happiness wherever they go;
others whenever they go.*

Light-As-A-Feather Sponge Cake

Great for strawberry shortcake.

2	eggs, separated	2
¼ tsp.	cream of tartar	1 mL
¼ cup	water	60 mL
3 tbsp.	oil	45 mL
½ cup	sugar	125 mL
¼ tsp.	salt	1 mL
⅔ cup	flour	150 mL
1 tsp.	baking powder	5 mL

- Preheat oven to 325°F (160°C).
- In a small mixing bowl, beat egg whites and cream of tartar until stiff. Set aside.
- In another small mixing bowl, beat egg yolks, water, oil, sugar and salt until thick and light in color, about 3 minutes.
- Mix flour and baking powder together and slowly stir into egg yolk mixture.
- Gently fold egg whites into mixture.
- Pour into a greased and floured 9" (23 cm) round or square cake pan or pie plate.
- Bake for 40-45 minutes.
- Serve with fruit such as blueberries or strawberries and whipped cream.

Yield: 9" (23 cm) cake.

Hint: *For easy removal of cake from pan, line bottom of pan with waxed paper. All you have to do when the cake is done baking is loosen sides with a knife and invert. Cake pops out easily. Remember to pull waxed paper off cake before topping with fruit and/or whipped cream.*

Chocolate Cream Cake

This cake also makes a great Black Forest Cake. This is a very moist cake and slightly heavier than the Old-Fashioned Chocolate Cake.

2¼ cups	sifted flour	550 mL
2 tsp.	baking soda	10 mL
½ tsp.	salt	2 mL
½ cup	butter OR margarine, softened	125 mL
2 cups	firmly packed light brown sugar	500 mL
3	eggs	3
3 x 1 oz.	squares unsweetened chocolate (¾-1 cup [175-250 mL] semisweet chocolate pieces may be used)	3 x 30 g
1½ tsp.	vanilla	7 mL
1 cup	sour cream (buttermilk OR yogurt may be substituted)	250 mL
1 cup	boiling water	250 mL

- Preheat oven to 350°F (180°C).
- Grease and flour 2, 9" (23 cm) or 3, 8" (20 cm) round cake pans or 1, 9 x 13" (23 x 33 cm) pan.
- Sift together flour, baking soda and salt.
- In a large mixing bowl, beat butter, sugar and eggs on high speed until light and fluffy.
- Melt chocolate in the microwave on low or over hot water in a double boiler.
- Beat vanilla and melted chocolate into sugar mixture.
- Stir in dry ingredients, alternating with sour cream, and beating with a spoon until smooth.
- Stir in water. This will be a thin batter.
- Pour batter into prepared baking pans and bake approximately 30 minutes, or until centers spring back when pushed lightly with a fingertip or a toothpick inserted in the center comes out clean.
- Cool 10 minutes then invert on racks.
- If 2 pans were used, split each layer in half horizontally. Fill and frost with either a whipped cocoa cream topping or a Cooked Frosting, page 153.

Yield: A 2- or 3-layer cake.

Hint: *For easier frosting, place any cake in the freezer for 2 hours before frosting.*

Old-Fashioned Chocolate Cake

This moist light-textured cake is simple for beginners.

½ cup	melted shortening OR oil	125 mL
1½ cups	sugar	375 mL
2	eggs	2
1 tsp.	vanilla	5 mL
½ cup	milk	125 mL
2 tsp.	baking soda	10 mL
½ cup	cocoa	125 mL
2½ cups	flour	625 mL
½ tsp.	salt	2 mL
1 cup	boiling water	250 mL

- In a large bowl, combine oil, sugar, eggs, vanilla, milk and baking soda.
- In a medium mixing bowl, combine cocoa, flour and salt.
- Add dry ingredients to wet ingredients and beat well.
- Add boiling water to batter and beat until smooth.
- Pour batter into 2 greased and floured 9" (23 cm) layer baking pans or 1, 9 x 13" (23 x 33 cm) pan. Bake at 350°F (180°C) for 25-30 minutes.
- Fill and frost with your favorite icing.

Yield: 9" (23 cm) layer cake.

Variation:
Black Forest Cake:

- Use 1 round 9" (23 cm) chocolate layer; freeze the other one.
- Split cake in half horizontally to make 2 thin layers.
- Put half on plate and spread with cherry pie filling. Top with other half.
- Whip 1 cup (250 mL) of whipping cream. Add ¼ cup (60 mL) icing sugar and ½ tsp. (2 mL) vanilla.
- Remove ½ cup (125 mL) of sweetened whipped cream and set aside for garnish. Add 1 tbsp. (15 mL) sifted cocoa to remaining whipped cream and whisk until well blended. Spread chocolate cream all over cake.
- With an icing bag or teaspoon, place 8 dollops of reserved cream next to each other in a circle around the top of cake; put a dollop in the middle of the cake.
- Place a maraschino cherry in the middle of each dollop of cream.
- Shave a chocolate bar with a potato peeler or razor to make chocolate curls.
- Sprinkle these liberally all over the cake.

Variation: *If you want a taller cake, use 2, 9" (23 cm) chocolate cakes and make 4 layers.*

Cooked Frosting

The creamiest frosting you'll ever make.

⅓ cup	flour	75 mL
1 cup	milk	250 mL
1 cup	butter OR margarine	250 mL
1 cup	sugar	250 mL
1 tsp.	vanilla	5 mL

- In a double boiler, cook flour and milk together until thick, stirring constantly to prevent scorching. The microwave may also be used. Cook on high for 30 seconds then stir and repeat until the mixture is quite thick, like a paste. It will look like sticky mashed potatoes.
- Let this mixture cool in the refrigerator, covered with waxed paper or plastic wrap.
- Cream together butter, sugar and vanilla. Beat on high until very light and fluffy, up to 5 minutes, scraping sides often.
- Add the cooled flour mixture to the creamed mixture and beat until smooth and creamy. Any sugar crystals will dissolve within 20 minutes.

Yield: Frosting for 1, 9 x 13" (23 x 33 cm) cake or 1, 9" (23 cm) layer cake.

Variations:

Chocolate Frosting: *Add 2 tbsp. (30 mL) cocoa during the flour-milk stage.*

Mock Cream *Instead of using milk, use 1 cup (250 mL) plain yogurt.*
Cheese Frosting: *The frosting will taste surprisingly like cream cheese frosting.*

Hint: *Flavors can be varied as well as color, just use flavoring extracts instead of vanilla and tint with food colorings if you wish.*

Chocolate Buttercream Frosting

Great on brownies.

⅓ cup	butter OR margarine, softened	75 mL
1 tsp.	vanilla	5 mL
⅓ cup	cocoa	75 mL
2½ cups	icing sugar	625 mL
¼ cup	milk OR water	60 mL

- In a medium-sized mixing bowl, beat butter until light and fluffy.
- Add vanilla and cocoa and beat until smooth.
- Add icing sugar and milk alternately and beat until fluffy.
- Spread on cake.

Yield: Enough for a 9" (23 cm) cake.

Royal Icing

The best for gingerbread houses, this holds like glue.

2	egg whites	2
3¼ cups	icing sugar	800 mL
1 tsp.	vanilla	5 mL
½ tsp.	cream of tartar	2 mL

- In a medium-sized mixing bowl, combine all ingredients.
- Beat for 8 minutes with an electric mixer, until stiff.
- Use for decorating gingerbread houses or for making decorations, such as flowers, for cakes.

Yield: 2 cups (500 mL).

Hint: *Keep frosting covered with a lid or a damp cloth or it will dry out and harden.*

Cream Cheese Frosting

4 oz.	pkg. cream cheese, softened	125 g
¼ cup	butter	60 mL
1 tsp.	vanilla	5 mL
2 cups	icing sugar	500 mL

- In a medium-sized bowl, beat cream cheese and butter until light and fluffy.
- Add vanilla and beat again.
- Add icing sugar a little at a time and beat until smooth and fluffy.
- Spread over a 9" (23 cm) square or round cake.

Yield: Enough for 1, 9" (23 cm) cake.

Variation: *Try Mock Cream Cheese Frosting, page 153.*

Note: *This can be doubled for a layer or 9 x 13" (23 x 33 cm) cake.*

Buttercream Frosting

¼ cup	butter	60 mL
2½ cups	icing sugar	625 mL
1 tsp.	vanilla	5 mL
2 tbsp.	milk	30 mL

- In a small bowl, beat butter and half of the icing sugar.
- Add vanilla and milk. Beat until smooth.
- Add remaining icing sugar a little bit at a time until the desired consistency is reached.

Yield: Enough for 1, 9" (23 cm) cake.

Elegant Chocolate Cheesecake

This cheesecake tastes just as good as it looks.

Crust:

1½ cups	chocolate wafer crumbs	375 mL
¼ cup	melted butter	60 mL

Filling:

2 x 8 oz.	pkgs. cream cheese, softened	2 x 250 g
½ cup	sugar	125 mL
3	eggs	3
4 x 1 oz.	squares semisweet chocolate OR ½ cup (125 mL) semisweet chocolate pieces, melted	4 x 30 g

Topping:

4 x 1 oz.	squares semisweet chocolate, melted	4 x 30 g
½ cup	sour cream	125 mL

- For the crust, mix wafer crumbs with melted butter. Spread over sides and bottom of a 10" (25 cm) springform pan or a large pie plate.
- Preheat oven to 325°F (160°C).
- In a large mixing bowl, beat cream cheese until softened.
- Add sugar and eggs, 1 at a time. Mix until well blended, 2-3 minutes.
- In a double boiler or microwave, melt chocolate.
- Add chocolate to cream cheese mixture and mix until thick and smooth.
- Pour into prepared crust.
- Bake for 30-35 minutes, until firm in center.
- Chill 4 hours or overnight.
- Melt chocolate for topping in same manner as for cheesecake.
- Stir in sour cream and spread over top of cheesecake.
- Chill until firm.

Yield: 12" (30 cm) cheesecake.

Variations: *The top of the cheesecake may be decorated with whipped cream. Fresh fruit sauces, e.g., raspberry or cherry, or pie fillings and dollops of whipped cream also make delicious toppings.*

Dessert

Blueberry Cheesecake Torte, page 161

Baked Cheesecake

*This basic cake may be topped with any variety of fruit toppings or you may
sprinkle leftover crumb mixtures over the cheesecake. When you are in a hurry,
cherry or blueberry pie filling makes a delicious and easy topping.*

Crust:

1½ cups	graham cracker crumbs	375 mL
¼ cup	melted butter	60 mL
¼ cup	sugar	60 mL

Filling:

2 x 8 oz.	cream cheese	2 x 250 g
2	eggs	2
½ cup	sugar	125 mL
1 tsp.	vanilla	5 mL

Topping:

2 cups	sour cream	500 mL
1 tsp.	vanilla	5 mL
½ cup	sugar	125 mL

- In a 10" (25 cm) springform pan or a large pie plate, combine the graham cracker crumbs, sugar and melted butter. Mix well.
- Press crumb mixture over the bottom and sides of the pie pan. If using a springform pan, press onto the bottom of the pan reserving any excess crumbs.
- In a large mixing bowl, beat cream cheese until softened. Add eggs, 1 at a time, sugar and vanilla; mix until well blended.
- Pour cream cheese mixture into prepared crust. Bake for 25 minutes at 325°F (160°C), or until center is set. Remove cake from oven.
- Combine topping ingredients and pour over cheesecake. Bake at 400°F (200°C) for 4 minutes.
- Remove and cool for approximately 1 hour. Refrigerate until firm.

Serves 12-14.

Strawberry Topping

¾ cup	diced strawberries	175 mL
½ cup	water	125 mL
⅓ cup	sugar	75 mL
1 tbsp.	cornstarch	15 mL

- In a small saucepan, combine all ingredients. Bring to a boil and cook until thick and clear.

Blueberry Cheesecake Torte

This takes time to make but it is worth the effort.

Base:

2	eggs, separated	2
¼ tsp.	cream of tartar	1 mL
¼ cup	water	60 mL
3 tbsp.	oil	45 mL
½ cup	sugar	125 mL
¼ tsp.	salt	1 mL
⅔ cup	all-purpose flour	150 mL
1 tsp.	baking powder	5 mL

Filling:

3 tbsp.	sugar	45 mL
1 tbsp.	cornstarch	15 mL
1 tbsp.	all-purpose flour	15 mL
⅛ tsp.	salt	0.5 mL
⅔ cup	milk	150 mL
1	egg	1
1 cup	whipping cream, whipped	250 mL
1 tsp.	vanilla	5 mL
¼ oz.	pkg. unflavored gelatin (1 tbsp. [15 mL])	7 g
¼ cup	cold water	60 mL
¼ cup	boiling water	60 mL
8 oz.	pkg. cream cheese	250 g

- Preheat oven to 325°F (160°C).
- To make the base, in a small bowl, beat egg whites and cream of tartar until stiff. Set aside.
- In another bowl, beat egg yolks, water, oil, sugar and salt until thick and light in color, about 3 minutes.
- Mix flour and baking powder together. Slowly stir flour and baking powder into egg yolk mixture.
- Gently fold egg whites into egg yolk mixture.
- Pour into a greased and floured 9" (23 cm) springform pan.
- Bake for 30 minutes, or until a toothpick comes out clean.
- Place pan on cooling rack. DO NOT INVERT CAKE. Keep in pan.
- To make filling, in a small saucepan, combine sugar, cornstarch, flour and salt.
- Gradually stir in milk. Whisk together until completely mixed.
- Cook over medium heat, stirring constantly until thick and bubbly.

Blueberry Cheesecake Torte

Continued

- Stir half of the hot mixture into the slightly beaten egg and whisk until smooth. Pour back into the rest of the hot mixture and cook, stirring constantly, until it comes to a boil again.
- Cool in the refrigerator or freezer until cold.
- Meanwhile, whip cream with vanilla and set aside.
- In a measuring cup or cereal bowl, sprinkle gelatin over the cold water to dissolve. Add boiling water and stir. Set aside.
- In a medium-sized mixing bowl, beat cream cheese until light.
- Add cooled custard mixture and gelatin to cream cheese and beat until smooth.
- Fold in whipped cream. Pour cream cheese mixture over cooled cake in pan.
- Refrigerate, covered, for at least 2 hours.
- Prepare Blueberry Topping below.
- When cool, spread blueberry mixture evenly over cream cheese filling.
- Return to refrigerator.
- When set, slice to serve. This freezes very well.

Yield: 9" (23 cm) cheesecake.

Blueberry Topping

2 cups	fresh OR frozen blueberries	500 mL
2 tbsp.	butter	30 mL
2/3 cup	sugar	150 mL
1/4 cup	cold water	60 mL
2 tbsp.	cornstarch	30 mL

- In a medium-sized saucepan, combine blueberries, butter and sugar.
- Bring to a boil, over medium heat, stirring constantly.
- Stir until sugar dissolves. Occasionally mash a few berries against the sides of the pot.
- In a measuring cup, stir water and cornstarch together.
- Pour into blueberry mixture; continue to cook until thick and bubbly.
- Remove from heat. Cool, stirring occasionally.

Variations: *Instead of blueberries use your favorite fruit, such as strawberry, peach, cherry.*

Topping may be spooned over or under individual servings.

See photograph on page 157.

Miniature Cheesecakes

Perfect for showers or receptions.

| 24 | paper OR foil cupcake liners | 24 |
| 24 | vanilla wafers, OR Graham Wafer Crust (see below) | 24 |

Filling:

2 x 8 oz.	pkgs. cream cheese, at room temperature	2 x 250 g
3	eggs	3
¾ cup	sugar	175 mL
2 tbsp.	lemon juice	30 mL

Topping:

whipped cream OR cream-type topping
fresh fruit (strawberries, kiwi, blueberries),
  cherry pie filling, etc.

- Place medium cupcake liners in 24 muffin cups. Place a vanilla wafer, flat side down in the bottom of each liner OR make graham crust and place 1½ tbsp. (22 mL) of crumb mixture in bottom of each cupcake liner. Flatten crumb mixture with a small glass and set aside.
- To prepare filling, in a medium-sized mixing bowl, beat cream cheese, eggs, sugar and lemon juice until smooth and creamy.
- Preheat oven to 325°F (160°C).
- Fill each cupcake liner with at least 2 tbsp. (30 mL) filling or ¾ full.
- Bake for 20-25 minutes. Remove from oven and chill.
- Top with whipped cream and place a few pieces of fruit on top of whipped cream or spoon canned pie filling on top.

Yield: 24 miniature cheesecakes.

Graham Wafer Crust

1½ cups	graham wafer crumbs	375 mL
¼ cup	brown sugar	60 mL
⅓ cup	butter, melted	75 mL

- To make crust, mix crumbs, sugar and melted butter together. Mix evenly to coat crumbs.

Variation: *Apple, Peach and Lemon Danish Fillings, page 29, are excellent toppings.*

Miniature Cheesecakes

Continued

Miniature Black Forest Cheesecakes

Crust — omit sugar and substitute chocolate wafer crumbs for graham crumbs OR use chocolate wafers.

Filling — beat together 2 x 8 oz. (2 x 250 g) pkgs. cream cheese, ¹/₂ cup (125 mL) sugar, 3 eggs, ¹/₂ cup (125 mL) melted chocolate chips.

Topping — whipped cream and cherry pie filling or maraschino cherries.

Creamy Frozen Lemon Mousse

This is a nice light dessert. It is refreshing after a heavy meal.

6	eggs, separated	6
¹/₂ cup	lemon juice	125 mL
2 tsp.	grated lemon rind	10 mL
¹/₃ cup	sugar	75 mL
¹/₄ tsp.	cream of tartar	1 mL
³/₄ cup	sugar	175 mL
2 cups	whipping cream, whipped	500 mL
	fresh fruit for garnish	
	whipped cream for garnish	

- In a small bowl, beat egg yolks, lemon juice, lemon rind and ¹/₃ cup (75 mL) sugar together until light. Set aside.
- Beat egg whites and cream of tartar until almost stiff.
- Beat ³/₄ cup (175 mL) sugar into egg whites, a little at a time, until stiff and satiny.
- Fold the egg whites into the egg yolk mixture.
- Fold the whipped cream into the egg mixture. Pour into a lightly greased 9 x 13" (23 x 33 cm) pan. Cover and freeze until firm.
- Just before serving, add a dollop of whipped cream to each serving then place a piece of fresh fruit on top of the cream. Blueberry Sauce, page 14, is very good drizzled on top.

Serves 12.

Cream Cheese Pineapple Delight

This recipe has the flavor of a cheesecake but the texture of Pineapple Delight, a nice light dessert.

1¼ cups	graham wafer crumbs	300 mL
¼ cup	butter, melted	60 mL
¼ cup	brown sugar	60 mL
1 cup	whipping cream, whipped	250 mL
1 cup	boiling water	250 mL
3 oz.	pkg. pineapple OR lemon gelatin	85 g
8 oz.	pkg. cream cheese, softened	250 g
¼ cup	icing sugar	60 mL
14 oz.	can crushed pineapple, drained	398 mL
½ cup	thinly sliced blanched almonds, roasted	125 mL

- Preheat oven to 350°F (180°C).
- In a small bowl, stir graham wafer crumbs, butter and brown sugar together until well blended.
- Press into a 9" (23 cm) square baking pan or a 9" (23 cm) round springform pan.
- Bake for 7 minutes.
- Remove from oven, cool and set aside.
- Beat whipping cream. Set aside.
- In a small bowl or large measuring cup pour boiling water over gelatin and stir until dissolved. Set aside.
- In a large mixing bowl, beat cream cheese and icing sugar until light and fluffy.
- Pour in gelatin mixture and beat until smooth.
- Stir in drained pineapple; fold in whipped cream; pour over cooled crust and sprinkle with almonds.
- Refrigerate for 2-3 hours.
- Slice and serve.

Serves 12.

Variations:

Mandarin Delight: *Use orange gelatin and substitute canned mandarin oranges for pineapple.*

Strawberry Delight: *Use strawberry gelatin and 1 cup (250 mL) fresh or frozen sliced strawberries instead of pineapple.*

Oreo Ice Cream

A delicious ice cream treat that does not need an ice cream maker.

4	eggs, separated	4
²⁄₃ cup	icing sugar	150 mL
1 tsp.	vanilla	5 mL
1½ cups	whipping cream	375 mL
½ cup	Oreo crumbs	125 mL

- In a medium-sized bowl, beat egg whites until stiff peaks form.
- Gradually beat in icing sugar.
- Beat in egg yolks, 1 at a time.
- Beat in vanilla; set aside.
- In a large bowl, beat whipping cream until it holds its shape.
- Fold whipped cream into egg mixture.
- Stir in Oreo crumbs.
- Pour into a 2-quart (2 L) plastic container with a lid.
- Freeze for 8 hours, or until evenly frozen.

Yield: 1½ **quarts (1.5 L).**

Ice Cream Sandwiches

These are easy to make and children love to make and eat them.

1	recipe of any of the following cookies OR any of your own favorite cookie recipes; Deep Chocolate — Chocolate Chip Cookies, page 135, Peanut Butter Oatmeal Cookies (page 132), Chocolate Chip Cookies (page 134), Grandma's Ginger Cookies (page 128), Grandma's Sugar Cookies (page 129) vanilla ice cream, softened	1

- Make cookies according to recipe instructions.
- If you want big ice cream sandwiches, make dough balls 2" (5 cm) in diameter and flatten.
- When cookies are baked and cooled, take 1 cookie and spread with ice cream, as thick as you like. Place another cookie on top.
- Place in freezer container in deep-freeze until ready to eat and enjoy.

Yield: As many as you like.

Basic Cooked Pudding

Smooth and creamy — why pay the high price of the commercial brands when the results of this recipe are better and you can make an infinite variety of flavors.

¾ cup	sugar	175 mL
5 tbsp.	cornstarch	75 mL
3 cups	cold milk	750 mL
2	eggs, slightly beaten	2
1 tsp.	vanilla	5 mL
1 tbsp.	butter	15 mL

- In a medium saucepan, combine sugar and cornstarch. Gradually add milk and whisk until smooth. Cook over medium heat, stirring constantly, until thickened and mixture coats a metal spoon.
- In a small bowl or measuring cup, beat eggs lightly. Add 1 cup (250 mL) of the hot mixture to eggs and stir quickly, then pour egg mixture back into pudding and whisk to blend. Stir over medium heat for 1 minute and remove from heat. Stir in vanilla and butter. Cool for five minutes, stirring occasionally.
- Pour into dessert dishes.
- Top with your favorite fresh fruit, shaved chocolate and/or a dollop of whipped cream.

Makes 6, ½ cup (125 mL) servings.

Variations:

Chocolate: *Add ⅓ cup (75 mL) of cocoa to cornstarch and sugar. Increase sugar to 1 cup (250 mL).*

Butterscotch: *Use 1 cup (250 mL) brown sugar instead of white sugar. Add 3 tbsp. (45 mL) butter at end.*

Coconut: *Add ¾ cup (175 mL) shredded coconut.*

Banana: *Add 3 sliced bananas to warm pudding. Banana extract can be used instead of vanilla.*

Lemon: *Add 1 tsp. (5 mL) lemon extract instead of vanilla and ½ tsp. (2 mL) grated lemon rind.*

Pudding Pie Filling: *To use any of these puddings for a pie filling, add 1 more egg.*

Traditional Rice Pudding

This recipe is just like the one Grandma used to make.

2 cups	cold precooked rice	500 mL
2 cups	milk	500 mL
½ cup	evaporated milk	125 mL
2 tbsp.	cornstarch	30 mL
¼ tsp.	salt	1 mL
½ cup	sugar	125 mL
2	eggs	2
½ cup	raisins	125 mL
¼ tsp.	cinnamon	1 mL
1 tsp.	vanilla	5 mL
dash	nutmeg	dash

- Cook rice and cool.
- In a medium saucepan, combine cold milks, cornstarch, salt and sugar.
- Stir over medium heat until thickened.
- Slightly beat eggs. Pour a bit of the thickened milk mixture into the eggs and whisk thoroughly. Pour back into hot mixture, stirring constantly.
- Add raisins and cook for 1 more minute stirring constantly. Stir in rice.
- Remove from heat and add cinnamon, vanilla and nutmeg.
- Serve warm or cold.

Yield: 8, ½ cup (125 mL) servings.

He who takes but never gives
may last for years but never lives.

Heavenly Rice Pudding

The creamiest rice pudding you will ever taste.

2 cups	milk	500 mL
⅔ cup	uncooked rice	150 mL
1 tbsp.	butter	15 mL
¼ oz.	env. unflavored gelatin (1 tbsp. [15 mL])	7 g
¼ cup	cold water	60 mL
⅓ cup	sugar	75 mL
1 tsp.	vanilla	5 mL
⅛ tsp.	salt	0.5 mL
¼ tsp.	cinnamon	1 mL
¼ cup	chopped dried apricots (optional)	60 mL
⅓ cup	raisins (optional)	75 mL
¼ cup	chopped almonds (optional)	60 mL
2 cups	whipping cream, whipped	500 mL

- In a medium-sized saucepan, bring milk to a boil and reduce heat to medium-low.
- Add rice and butter. Simmer, covered, until rice is cooked (30 minutes).
- Dissolve gelatin in water. Stir gelatin mixture into rice and milk.
- Add sugar, vanilla, salt, cinnamon and dried apricots or raisins.
- Cool to room temperature, stirring occasionally.
- Fold in whipped cream and almonds.
- Refrigerate for 2 hours.
- If fruit or nuts have not been added, top with a teaspoon (5 mL) of your favorite jam or maple syrup.

Serves 6-8.

Caramel-Apple Pudding Cake

Serve warm. This is very good with a scoop of ice cream.

1 cup	flour	250 mL
2 tsp.	baking powder	10 mL
¼ tsp.	salt	1 mL
½ cup	sugar	125 mL
½ tsp.	cinnamon	2 mL
¼ tsp.	nutmeg	1 mL
1	medium apple, peeled, cored and diced	1
½ cup	milk	125 mL
1¾ cups	boiling water	425 mL
2 tbsp.	butter	30 mL
1 cup	brown sugar	250 mL

- Preheat oven to 350°F (180°C).
- Combine the first 6 ingredients in a medium bowl.
- Add apples and stir to coat with dry mixture.
- Stir in milk.
- Pour and spread in a greased 9" (23 cm) square pan.
- Combine boiling water, butter and brown sugar.
- Stir to dissolve sugar and melt butter.
- Carefully pour sugar mixture over batter.
- Bake for 45 minutes.
- To serve, spoon pudding over cake.

Serves 6-8.

Fruit Crisp Desserts

Make with your favorite fruit in season. Try some of these variations or experiment with your own combinations. All are good with a scoop of vanilla ice cream.

Crispy Topping:

½ cup	flour (all-purpose OR whole-wheat)	125 mL
¾ cup	rolled oats	175 mL
⅓ cup	brown sugar	75 mL
½ tsp.	salt	2 mL
½ tsp.	cinnamon	2 mL
⅓ cup	butter OR margarine	75 mL
2 tbsp.	finely chopped walnuts (optional)	30 mL

Rhubarb Crisp Filling:

2 tbsp.	water	30 mL
4 cups	sliced rhubarb	1 L
¾ cup	sugar	175 mL
2 tbsp.	flour	30 mL
½ tsp.	cinnamon	2 mL

- To make the topping, combine all dry ingredients in a small bowl and rub butter into dry mixture until it resembles coarse crumbs.
- Stir in walnuts, if used. Sprinkle over prepared fruit filling.
- Preheat oven to 350°F (180°C).
- To prepare the filling, sprinkle water over rhubarb and toss.
- Combine sugar, flour and cinnamon.
- Stir flour mixture into rhubarb, mixing well.
- Pour into a greased 9" (23 cm) square pan.
- Sprinkle crispy topping evenly over rhubarb.
- Bake for 45 minutes.

Serves 10-12.

Apple Crisp Filling

4 cups	peeled, cored and sliced apples	1 L
1 tbsp.	lemon juice	15 mL
½ cup	sugar	125 mL
½ tsp.	cinnamon	2 mL
2 tbsp.	flour	30 mL

- Follow directions for Rhubarb Crisp.

170

Peach Crisp Filling

4 cups	sliced peaches (fresh OR canned)	1 L
1 tbsp.	lemon juice	15 mL
½ cup	white sugar, OR ¼ cup (60 mL) each white and brown sugar	125 mL
½ tsp.	cinnamon	2 mL
2 tbsp.	flour	30 mL

• Follow directions for Rhubarb Crisp.

Apple Cranberry Crisp Filling

2 cups	peeled, cored and sliced apples	500 mL
14 oz.	can wholeberry cranberry sauce	398 mL
¼ tsp.	cinnamon	1 mL
½ cup	sugar	125 mL
2 tbsp.	flour	30 mL

• Follow directions for Rhubarb Crisp.

See photograph on page 175.

Apple Rhubarb Crisp Filling

2½ cups	peeled, cored and sliced apples	625 mL
1½ cups	sliced rhubarb	375 mL
2 tbsp.	water	30 mL
¾ cup	sugar	175 mL
½ tsp.	cinnamon	2 mL
2 tbsp.	flour	30 mL

• Follow directions for Rhubarb Crisp.

Peach Blueberry Crisp Filling

3 cups	sliced peaches	750 mL
1 cup	blueberries	250 mL
½ cup	sugar	125 mL
1 tbsp.	lemon juice	15 mL
2 tbsp.	flour	30 mL
¼ tsp.	cinnamon	1 mL
¼ tsp.	mace	1 mL

• Follow directions for Rhubarb Crisp.

Lemon Sponge Pudding

An old-fashioned favorite that is equally good warm or cold.

3	eggs, separated	3
¾ cup	sugar	175 mL
⅓ cup	flour	75 mL
¼ cup	melted butter OR margarine	60 mL
½ tsp.	grated lemon peel	2 mL
¼ cup	lemon juice	60 mL
1½ cups	milk	375 mL

- Preheat oven to 350°F (180°C).
- Beat egg whites until stiff and set aside.
- In a large mixing bowl, combine sugar, flour, butter, lemon peel and lemon juice.
- Whisk together milk and egg yolks until frothy and add to sugar and lemon mixture. Stir to mix.
- Fold in egg whites.
- Pour into a 9" (23 cm) square baking pan.
- Place pan in a larger pan in oven and pour boiling water, about 1" (2.5 cm) deep, into the large pan.
- Bake for 40-45 minutes.
- Cut into 9 servings. Spoon pudding over cake.

Serves 9.

The only person who ever got his work done by Friday
was Robinson Crusoe.
(A.J. Marshall)

Hot Fudge Pudding Cake

If you don't mind the calories, top with a scoop of vanilla ice cream.

2 cups	flour	500 mL
1⅓ cups	white sugar	325 mL
¼ cup	cocoa	60 mL
1 tbsp.	baking powder	15 mL
½ tsp.	salt	2 mL
½ cup	chopped walnuts OR pecans	125 mL
1 cup	milk	250 mL
¼ cup	oil	60 mL
1 tsp.	vanilla	5 mL
3½ cups	hot water	875 mL
1½ cups	brown sugar	375 mL
½ cup	cocoa	125 mL

- Preheat oven to 350°F (180°C).
- In a large mixing bowl, combine flour, white sugar, ¼ cup (60 mL) cocoa, baking powder, salt and nuts.
- Add milk, oil and vanilla and stir until well mixed.
- Pour into a greased 9 x 13" (23 x 33 cm) pan. Spread to the edges.
- Combine water, brown sugar and cocoa and pour gently over cake batter.
- Bake for 35-40 minutes, or until cake tests done.
- To serve, spoon pudding over cake.

Yield: 12 large servings.

Banana Boats

This children's treat is also a hit with adults and a great dessert for camping.

bananas
chocolate chips
miniature marshmallows
foil wrap

- Slit banana down the middle lengthwise. DO NOT CUT THROUGH.
- Sprinkle chocolate chips down the middle.
- Place some marshmallows over the chocolate chips.
- Wrap in foil and bake in oven at 350°F (180°C) for 10 minutes. Do not overcook or bananas will turn to mush. You want them warm but firm.

Variation: *Roast foil packages at the edge of hot coals at a campfire.*

Perfect Pie Pastry

No more frisbees with this recipe.

1 cup	lard OR shortening	250 mL
½ cup	butter or margarine	125 mL
1 tsp.	salt	5 mL
3 cups	flour	750 mL
½ cup	cold water	125 mL

- In a large mixing bowl, beat lard and butter together.
- Add salt and mix well.
- Beat in 1 cup (250 mL) of flour.
- Add remaining flour, 1 cup (250 mL) at a time, creaming well with the back of a spoon with each addition.
- Add water all at once. With back of spoon, push flour mixture into the water evenly.
- Quickly form into a ball. This will be sticky so use plenty of flour when rolling out pastry.
- This pastry will roll out smoothly and will not fall to pieces.

Yield: Enough pastry for 2 double-crust pies.

Hint: *Roll dough between 2 sheets of floured waxed paper for less mess and greater ease in transferring pastry to pie plates.*

Tell the truth. Live the truth.
Live so that you don't have to remember what you said.

Dessert

Sweet Empanadas

These are great little pastries for fondues. They can be served as a sweet appetizer or as the finale to a special meal.

	pastry for a 9" (23 cm) pie shell, page 174	
½ cup	apricot jam	125 mL
1 cup	shredded coconut	250 mL
¼ cup	diced maraschino cherries, patted dry	60 mL
2 tbsp.	chopped pecans	30 mL
2 tbsp.	raisins	30 mL
1 tsp.	vanilla	5 mL
½ tsp.	cinnamon	2 mL
⅛ tsp.	nutmeg	0.5 mL
⅓ cup	sugar	75 mL
1½ tsp.	cinnamon	7 mL

- Prepare pastry.
- Preheat oil in a deep-fryer to 375°F (190°C).
- In a medium-sized bowl, combine all ingredients, except sugar and 1½ tsp. (7 mL) cinnamon.
- Roll pastry to ⅛" (3 mm) thickness and cut with a 3" (7 cm) round cookie cutter or a Mason jar lid.
- Place a teaspoon (5 mL) of filling on each pastry round.
- Fold in half, moisten edges with water, milk or egg white, then press edges together with a fork.
- Combine sugar and cinnamon in a bag and set aside.
- Drop each empanada into the deep hot fat until pastry is golden brown. Turn pastries as the first side browns.
- Drain on paper toweling then coat with sugar and cinnamon mixture.

Yield: 4-5 dozen Empanadas.

Variation: *For a lower-fat version, these can also be baked in the oven at 400°F (200°C). Brush with milk and sprinkle with cinnamon and sugar before baking.*

Lemon Meringue Pie

This pie has a very mellow flavor.

9" (23 cm) pie shell, OR 12 unbaked tart shells

1¼ cups	sugar	300 mL
⅓ cup	cornstarch	75 mL
1⅔ cups	cold water	400 mL
3	egg yolks (save whites for meringue, below)	3
⅓ cup	lemon juice	75 mL
2 tsp.	grated lemon rind	10 mL
½ tsp.	lemon extract	2 mL
3 tbsp.	butter	45 mL
	yellow food coloring (optional)	

- Prepare pastry.
- In the top of a double boiler, combine sugar and cornstarch.
- Add water and mix with a whisk until the cornstarch is dissolved.
- Cook over boiling water, stirring constantly until thick and clear.
- In a measuring cup, beat egg yolks and pour a bit of the hot mixture into the egg yolks. Mix well and pour back into the cornstarch mixture in the double boiler, stirring all the while.
- Cook, stirring constantly for 1 more minute.
- Remove from heat and stir in lemon juice, lemon rind and lemon extract.
- Add butter and food coloring, if using.
- Cool for 15 minutes, stirring occasionally. Pour into a baked pie shell.
- Cool until lukewarm, then preheat oven to 350°F (180°C) and spread meringue over pie filling, making sure that meringue touches all edges of the crust.
- Bake for 8-10 minutes, or until meringue is golden.
- Cool completely before serving.

Yield: 1, 9" (23 cm) pie OR 12 tarts.

Meringue

3	egg whites	3
⅓ cup	sugar	75 mL
¼ tsp.	cream of tartar	1 mL

- Beat egg whites until light and fluffy. Gradually add cream of tartar and sugar; beat until stiff peaks form. For an extra-high meringue add 1 more egg white.

Hint: *When making single crust, prebaked pie shells, prick dough with a fork in uniform rows around edges and across the bottom. The crust will keep its shape better for filling.*

Blueberry Peach Pie

The flavors of blueberry and peach complement each other well.

	pastry for 9" (23 cm) double-crust pie, page 174	
4 cups	peeled, sliced peaches	1 L
1 cup	sugar	250 mL
⅓ cup	cornstarch	75 mL
¼ tsp.	cinnamon	1 mL
1 tbsp.	lemon juice	15 mL
1 cup	blueberries, fresh OR frozen	250 mL
	butter	

- Prepare pastry and line pie pan.
- Preheat oven to 350°F (180°C).
- To prepare peaches, dip in boiling water for 30 seconds. Dip in cold water and slip off skins. Slice thinly and put in a medium-sized bowl.
- Combine sugar, cornstarch and cinnamon. Pour over peaches and sprinkle with lemon juice. Stir and let sit to blend for 10 minutes.
- Gently stir in blueberries.
- Pour into an uncooked pastry shell and dot with butter.
- Cover with top crust, pinching sides to seal.
- With a knife, cut several slits in a decorative pattern in the crust for ventilation.
- Bake for 1 hour.

Yield: 1 pie.

Hint: *Place a baking sheet or a large piece of foil under the pie because it is juicy and may boil over.*

Apple-Rhubarb Pie

If Rhubarb Pie is too tart for you, try this one. The apples give it a milder flavor.

	pastry for a 9" (23 cm) double-crust pie, page 174	
2 cups	chopped rhubarb	500 mL
3 cups	sliced apples	750 mL
1⅓ cups	sugar	325 mL
½ tsp.	cinnamon	2 mL
⅓ cup	flour	75 mL
	butter	

- Prepare pastry and line pie pan.
- In a large bowl, toss rhubarb and sliced apples together.
- In a smaller bowl, combine sugar, cinnamon and flour.
- Sprinkle sugar mixture over fruit; stir and toss to coat.
- Let stand 15-20 minutes then stir again.
- Preheat oven to 350°F (180°C).
- Pour filling into pastry-lined pan. Dot filling with butter.
- Fit top crust over and seal edges tightly.
- Cut some slits in top in a decorative pattern for ventilation.
- Brush top crust with milk and sprinkle with sugar.
- Bake for 50 minutes.
- Remove from oven and let set for 1 hour.
- Serve with a big scoop of vanilla ice cream.

Yield: 1 pie.

Variation:

Strawberry-Rhubarb Pie: *To make this very popular version, use 3 or 4 cups (750 mL-1 L) of rhubarb and 1 or 2 cups (250-500 mL) of sliced strawberries, 5 cups (1.25 L) of fruit in total. Use the same amount of sugar, cinnamon and flour as above.*

Butter Tarts

	pastry for 9" (23 cm) double-crust pie, page 174	
½ cup	raisins OR currants	125 mL
	boiling water	
2	eggs	2
1 cup	brown sugar	250 mL
¼ cup	corn syrup	60 mL
1 tsp.	vanilla OR rum extract	5 mL
½ cup	melted butter	125 mL

- Line 18 tart shells with pastry.
- In a small bowl, cover raisins with boiling water. Let stand 5 minutes then drain.
- Preheat oven to 375°F (190°C).
- In a large mixing bowl, beat eggs, brown sugar and corn syrup together until frothy.
- Beat in vanilla and melted butter until well mixed.
- Stir in raisins.
- Bake for 15-20 minutes, or until pastry is golden brown.

Yield: 18 tarts.

Variation:
Butter Pecan Tarts: *Substitute 1 cup (250 mL) of pecans for raisins.*

Note: *For a more syrupy tart, add only 1 egg instead of 2.*

The best angle from which to approach a problem is the try-angle.

Cream Puffs

½ cup	butter	125 mL
1 cup	boiling water	250 mL
1 cup	flour	250 mL
⅛ tsp.	salt	0.5 mL
4	eggs	4

- Place butter and water in a large saucepan.
- Bring to a boil and stir until butter melts.
- Add flour and salt all at once.
- Stir and cook over medium heat until a ball forms that pulls away from the sides of the pan.
- Remove from heat and cool for 10 minutes.
- Preheat oven to 400°F (200°C).
- Beat in eggs, 1 at a time, beating until smooth after each addition.
- Drop by large spoonfuls on a greased baking sheet, 2" (5 cm) apart.
- Bake for 25-30 minutes.
- Cool puffs on a rack and split in half.
- Remove any doughy membrane from the middle.
- Fill with whipped cream.
- Cover with top and sprinkle with icing sugar.

Yield: 10-12 Cream Puffs.

Chocolate Eclairs

- Pipe dough into 4" (10 cm) lengths.
- Bake as for cream puffs.
- When baked, split and fill with whipped cream.
- Replace top and drizzle with melted chocolate.

Yield: 12 Eclairs.

Lemon Puffs

- Fill with 1-2 tbsp. (15-30 mL) lemon pudding and pie filling, see page 166.
- Spoon whipped cream on top.
- Put lid on and sprinkle with icing sugar.

Yield: 10-12 Lemon Puffs.

Creamy Caramels

This is a recipe from my friend Dorothy Wolsey who makes excellent candy and chocolates. The flavor of these is much better than any you can buy.

1 cup	butter	250 mL
2 cups	brown sugar	500 mL
10 oz.	can sweetened condensed milk or Homemade Sweetened Condensed Milk, page 200	300 mL
1 cup	corn syrup, light OR dark	250 mL
⅛ tsp.	salt	0.5 mL
½ tsp.	vanilla	2 mL

- Combine all ingredients, except vanilla, in a large heavy saucepan.
- Cook, stirring constantly, over medium heat until firm-ball stage (240°F [115°C]) or desired thickness. Check by placing a bit of syrup at a time on a spoon and drop it into cold water, then feel the piece with your fingers to see if it is firm enough.
- It usually takes 30-35 minutes over medium-low heat. Stir constantly or it will scorch.
- Remove from heat and add vanilla.
- Pour into a buttered 9 x 13" (23 x 33 cm) pan. Do not scrape pan when pouring.
- Cool, cut into ¾" (3 cm) squares and wrap in waxed paper or in colored foil at Christmas time or dip in chocolate.

Yield: Approximately 200 Caramels.

Variations: *Substitute other flavorings for vanilla for different-flavored toffees. Try peppermint, rum extract or maple, etc. Chopped walnuts or pecans also make good additions.*

Christmas Divinity Fudge

This is a delicate candy and it looks pretty.

3 cups	sugar	750 mL
¾ cup	light corn syrup	175 mL
½ cup	water	125 mL
⅛ tsp.	salt	0.5 mL
2	egg whites	2
½ tsp.	vanilla	2 mL
½ tsp.	almond extract	2 mL
2	drops red food coloring	2
¼ cup	chopped maraschino cherries	60 mL
½ cup	chopped roasted almonds OR walnuts	125 mL

- In a buttered saucepan, combine sugar, corn syrup, water and salt.
- Stir well and bring to a boil over medium heat.
- Cover for 2 minutes to melt sugar crystals down the sides of the saucepan.
- Remove cover and cook without stirring to hard-ball stage (255-260°F [125-127°C]).
- Meanwhile, beat egg whites in a large bowl until stiff.
- When syrup is at 260°F (127°C) pour slowly in a fine, steady stream into the egg whites, while beating. DO NOT SCRAPE SAUCEPAN.
- Add vanilla, almond extract and food coloring.
- Beat until candy is thick and creamy and holds its shape (5 minutes).
- Stir in cherries and nuts.
- Drop from a teaspoon (5 mL) onto waxed paper.
- Serve within a week.

Yield: 3½ dozen pieces.

Buttery Almond Crunch

A tasty gift at Christmas.

1 cup	sugar	250 mL
¼ cup	water	60 mL
1 cup	butter (do not substitute margarine)	250 mL
¾ cup	chopped roasted almonds	175 mL
1½ cups	chocolate chips OR 12 oz. (350 g) milk chocolate	375 mL

- In a medium-sized saucepan, mix sugar, water and butter. Stir over medium-high heat until butter is melted. Cover and bring to a boil.
- Remove cover, stir in ¼ cup (60 mL) of the almonds.
- Stir and cook until hard-crack stage (300°F [150°C]) on candy thermometer.
- It will darken and smoke.
- Pour onto a greased baking sheet and quickly spread around to edges or as close to edges as you can get.
- Sprinkle ¾ cup (175 mL) chocolate chips evenly over hot almond candy.
- As the chocolate chips melt, spread over entire surface.
- Sprinkle ¼ cup (60 mL) finely chopped almonds over melted chocolate. Cool.
- Melt remaining ¾ cup (175 mL) chocolate chips.
- Invert cooled candy onto the counter top. Spread melted chocolate chips over entire surface and sprinkle with ¼ cup (60 mL) finely chopped almonds.
- Cool and break into bite-sized pieces.

Yield: 1 lb. (500 g) of candy.

Variations:

Almond Roca: *Do not add almonds to hot syrup. Cook to hard-crack stage and pour into greased small ice-cube trays. When cool, remove candy from ice-cube trays and dip in melted chocolate. Roll in finely chopped almonds. Wrap in colored florist's foil.*

Peanut Brittle

Buttery and Crunchy.

1 cup	white sugar	250 mL
½ cup	corn syrup	125 mL
¼ cup	water	60 mL
½ cup	hard butter OR margarine	125 mL
1½ cups	dry-roasted peanuts	375 mL
½ tsp.	baking soda	2 mL
¼ tsp.	vanilla	1 mL

- Grease a 10 x 15" (25 x 38 cm) pan with butter and set aside.
- In a large heavy 6-quart (1.5 L) kettle, combine sugar, corn syrup and water.
- Stir over medium heat until sugar dissolves.
- When mixture comes to a boil add butter and stir until it melts.
- Continue to boil without stirring until candy thermometer reaches 275°F (140°C), soft crack.
- Quickly stir in peanuts, stirring constantly until candy thermometer reaches 300°F (150°C), hard crack.
- Remove from heat.
- Quickly stir in baking soda and vanilla.
- Pour into a buttered pan and spread to edges.
- Cool and break into small pieces.

Yield: Approximately 1 lb. (500 g) of candy.

You can't put your foot in the same river twice.

Poppycock

An excellent gift to give at Christmas time.

½ cup	popcorn kernels	125 mL
1½ cups	blanched almonds	375 mL
1½ cups	pecan halves	375 mL
1 cup	dry roasted peanuts	250 mL
1 cup	butter	250 mL
1⅓ cups	sugar	325 mL
½ cup	corn syrup	125 mL
½ tsp.	cream of tartar	2 mL
½ tsp.	baking soda	2 mL
½ tsp.	vanilla	2 mL

- Pop corn kernels and remove any unpopped kernels.
- Pour popcorn into a large greased bowl or roaster.
- Place almonds and pecan halves on a baking sheet and roast in a 325°F (160°C) oven until almonds are lightly browned.
- Pour almonds, pecans and peanuts into the bowl with the popcorn; set aside.
- In a medium-sized heavy saucepan, combine butter, sugar, corn syrup and cream of tartar. Cook over medium heat until you have a firm, hard ball when dropped in cold water, 250°F (120°C) on candy thermometer, or about 5 minutes cooking time from the time it starts to boil.
- Quickly add baking soda and vanilla. Stir rapidly, it will foam up. Pour over popcorn and nut mixture. Stir with a greased wooden spoon to coat.
- Turn onto a greased counter top or into 2 large greased baking pans. Press down evenly.
- Break into chunks when cool.

Yield: About 4 quarts (4 L) of Poppycock.

Colored Candy Popcorn

Just bursting with flavor.

¾ cup	popcorn kernels	175 mL
¾ cup	butter OR margarine	175 mL
2 cups	sugar	500 mL
1 cup	white corn syrup	250 mL
2 x ¼ oz.	pkg. unsweetened Kool-Aid (any flavor)	2 x 6 g
½ tsp.	baking soda	2 mL

- Pop corn and set aside in a large greased roasting pan. Discard any unpopped kernels.
- In a large heavy saucepan, combine margarine, sugar and corn syrup.
- Bring to a boil stirring constantly over medium heat.
- Boil for 3 minutes.
- Stir in Kool-Aid.
- Remove from heat. Stir in baking soda.
- Pour over popcorn and stir to coat evenly.
- Pour into 2 greased 10 x 15" (25 x 38 cm) baking pans or a large roasting pan.
- Bake at 225°F (107°C) for 30 minutes. Stir every 10 minutes.
- Remove from oven and quickly spread on a greased counter top and separate.
- Cool and put into a container.

Yield: About 5 quarts (5 L).

Variations:

Black Licorice Popcorn: *Add 5-6 drops oil of anise and black food coloring. Try orange and black for Halloween treats.*

Rootbeer Popcorn: *Add 1-2 tbsp. (15-30 mL) of Hires Rootbeer extract to the syrup mixture when it is removed from the heat.*

Chewy Popcorn Balls: *Form balls right after syrup is poured over popcorn. Do not bake.*

Crackerjack Popcorn

This will remind you of the crackerjacks we all loved as kids.

1 cup	popcorn kernels	250 mL
1 cup	dry-roasted peanuts	250 mL
1 cup	butter OR margarine	250 mL
¼ cup	corn syrup	60 mL
¼ cup	molasses	60 mL
2 cups	brown sugar	500 mL
½ tsp.	baking soda	2 mL
½ tsp.	vanilla	2 mL

- Pop popcorn kernels. Remove all unpopped seeds.
- Pour popcorn into a large, greased roasting pan — add peanuts and set aside.
- In a large heavy saucepan, combine butter, corn syrup, molasses and sugar.
- Bring to a full rolling boil over medium-heat stirring constantly.
- Remove spoon and boil for another 5 minutes.
- Remove from heat and quickly stir in baking soda and vanilla.
- Pour syrup over popcorn and peanuts and stir with a greased spoon until the popcorn is coated.
- Pour into a greased roaster or 2, 10 x 15" (25 x 39 cm) greased baking pans.
- Place roaster in oven and bake at 225°F (107°C) for 30 minutes.
- Stir every 10 minutes to make sure mixture does not scorch.
- Remove from oven and pour onto a table or counter top.
- Separate pieces quickly as it cools and hardens.

Yield: About 6 quarts (6 L).

Variation:

Caramel Corn: *Omit molasses and peanuts, increase corn syrup to ¹/₂ cup (125 mL).*

Granola

This is full of fiber and tastes great too!

6 cups	rolled oats	1.5 L
1 cup	wheat germ	250 mL
1 cup	chopped slivered almonds	250 mL
½ cup	sunflower seeds	125 mL
1 cup	shredded coconut	250 mL
½ cup	brown sugar	125 mL
1 tsp.	cinnamon	5 mL
1 tsp.	salt	5 mL
½ cup	oil	125 mL
½ cup	water	125 mL
1 tsp.	vanilla OR almond extract	5 mL
¾ cup	finely chopped dried apricots	175 mL

- In a large mixing bowl, stir together first 8 ingredients until well mixed.
- In a small bowl, combine oil, water and vanilla.
- Pour wet ingredients over dry mixture and stir together until well blended.
- Pour mixture into a large ungreased baking pan or roaster.
- Bake at 250°F (120°C) for 1 hour, or until golden brown, stirring every 10 minutes.
- Remove from oven. Add dried apricots. Mix well. Cool.
- Transfer to an airtight container.
- Serve as a breakfast cereal with milk or as a topping on ice cream, yogurt or porridge. Also, see recipe for Granola Bars, page 139.

Yield: 10 cups (2.5 L).

Variations: *Add 1 cup (250 mL) walnuts, ¾ cup (175 mL) chopped dates and ¾ cup (175 mL) raisins OR 1 cup (250 mL) peanuts and ¾ cup (175 mL) broken banana chips OR any other dried fruit or nuts.*

Hint: *Use scissors to cut dried fruit into pieces.*

Pickles, Preserves & Sauces

Crunchy Dill Pickles

A mild tasting pickle with a big crunch.

7 lbs.	small pickling cucumbers	3 kg
16 cups	water	4 L
3 cups	vinegar	750 mL
⅔ cup	pickling salt	150 mL
¼ cup	sugar	60 mL
	fresh dill	
	garlic cloves	

- Wash and sterilize jars. Keep hot in a boiling water bath or a 225°F (107°C) oven.
- Wash cucumbers. If cucumbers are large cut into quarters lengthwise.
- Combine water, vinegar, salt and sugar in a large pot or Dutch oven.
- Bring to a boil and simmer brine over low heat until ready to use.
- Place 1 sliced garlic clove and 1 sprig of dill in each jar.
- Fill with cucumbers and add 1 more sprig of dill on top.
- Pour boiling brine over cucumbers and run a knife along the inside edge to get rid of air bubbles.
- Add more brine if necessary and leave ½" (1.3 cm) headspace.
- Fit lids and process jars in a boiling water bath for 20 minutes from the time the jars are immersed in the canner. Reduce heat to low.
- Remove jars from canner and leave upright and undisturbed on the counter until they are cooled and the seal is complete.

Yield: 7 quarts (7 L).

Note: *Let pickles sit in a cool place for at least 2 weeks before sampling.*

See photograph on the back cover.

Bread and Butter Pickles

A great picnic companion.

16 cups	thinly sliced, unpeeled cucumbers	4 L
5 cups	sliced onions	1.25 L
2	garlic cloves, minced	2
½ cup	pickling salt	125 mL
	cracked OR crushed ice	
6 cups	sugar	1.5 L
3 cups	vinegar	750 mL
2 tsp.	turmeric	10 mL
1 tsp.	celery seed	5 mL
2 tbsp.	mustard seed	30 mL

- Prepare jars.
- In a large bowl, combine cucumbers, garlic and onions.
- Stir in salt. Cover with cracked ice, distributing ice throughout the cucumbers.
- Cover and let sit for 3 hours.
- Drain.
- In a large kettle, make a syrup by combining sugar, vinegar, turmeric, celery seed and mustard seed.
- Heat until sugar is dissolved.
- Add cucumbers and bring to a boil.
- Simmer for 2 minutes.
- Pack into hot sterilized jars. Wipe rims and fit on lids.
- Process jars in a boiling water bath for 7 minutes.
- Remove from the canner and leave undisturbed on the counter to cool and complete the seal.

Yield: 8 pints — 8, 2-cup (500 mL) jars.

Note: *These can be used within a week.*

See photograph on the back cover.

Dilled Carrots

An attractive addition to any pickle platter.

5 lbs.	carrots	2.2 kg
12 cups	water	3 L
2 cups	vinegar	500 mL
½ cup	pickling salt	125 mL
¼ cup	sugar	60 mL
	garlic cloves	
	dillweed	

- Sterilize 5, 1-quart (1 L) sealers. Keep hot in a 225°F (107°C) oven or in a water bath canner full of boiling water.
- Scrub or peel carrots. Slice off ends. If carrots are finger-sized keep whole, if not cut into carrot sticks. Keep fresh in cold water.
- In a large kettle combine water, vinegar, salt and sugar. Bring to a full rolling boil. Reduce heat and keep simmering.
- Fill jars with carrots. Put 2 sprigs of dill in each jar, 1 at the top and 1 at the bottom. Add 1 sliced garlic clove to each jar.
- Fill each jar with boiling brine leaving ½" (1.3 cm) headspace at the top. Remove air bubbles by sliding a knife down the inside edges of the jar. Wipe rims and fit on lids.
- Process in a boiling water bath for 10 minutes.

Yield: 5, 1-quart (1 L) jars.

Variation: Substitute 1 tbsp. (15 mL) dill seed for fresh dill in each jar.

Note: Let pickles sit in a cool place for 2 weeks before sampling.

See photograph on the back cover.

Corn Relish

Delicious on hotdogs or hamburgers.

8 cups	fresh kernel corn, OR 2.2 lb. (1 kg) bag frozen corn	2 L
1	large onion, finely chopped	1
1 cup	finely chopped celery	250 mL
⅓ cup	minced red pepper	75 mL
⅓ cup	minced green pepper	75 mL
1⅓ cups	sugar	325 mL
1 tsp.	salt	5 mL
½ tsp.	celery seed	2 mL
1	garlic clove, minced	1
½ tsp.	mustard seed	2 mL
1 tsp.	ground turmeric	5 mL
2 tsp.	dry mustard	10 mL
¼ tsp.	ground ginger	1 mL
3¼ cups	vinegar	800 mL
¾ cup	cold water	175 mL
¼ cup	cornstarch	60 mL

- Prepare jars as on page 192.
- In a large kettle or Dutch oven, combine everything except water and cornstarch.
- Bring to a boil over medium heat, stirring constantly.
- Reduce heat to medium-low and simmer for 10 minutes, or until onion and celery are tender. Stir occasionally.
- Combine water and cornstarch and mix until no lumps remain.
- Pour into the hot mixture and stir to mix.
- Simmer, stirring constantly, until thick and bubbly, 5-8 minutes.
- Pour into hot sterilized jars. Seal and process jars in a boiling water bath for 15 minutes.

Yield: 3½ pints — 7 cups (1.75 L) of relish.

Note: *This can be used immediately.*

See photograph on the back cover.

Mild Salsa

A great way to preserve a bumper crop of tomatoes.

15 lbs.	tomatoes, peeled and chopped (20 cups [5 L])	6.5 kg
5	fresh jalapeño peppers (save seeds from 2)	5
8-10 cups	chopped onions	2-2.5 L
2	large sweet green peppers, finely chopped	2
2 cups	vinegar	500 mL
13 oz.	can tomato paste	369 mL
1 tbsp.	pickling salt	15 mL
1	garlic clove, minced	1
½ cup	sugar	125 mL
1 tsp.	black pepper	5 mL
¼ tsp.	cumin	1 mL
1 tsp.	chili powder	5 mL
¼ tsp.	cayenne	1 mL
¾ cup	cold water	175 mL
½ cup	cornstarch	125 mL

- Prepare 14 pint (2-cup [500 mL]) jars.
- Place whole tomatoes in boiling water for 30 seconds or until skins split.
- Remove tomatoes with a slotted spoon and place in ice-cold water. Slip off skins.
- Core and dice tomatoes and place in a very large kettle.
- Using gloves, dice jalapeño peppers. Save seeds from 2 peppers and add to the pot with the peppers.
- Add seeds of 2 jalapeños peppers to pot.
- Add remaining ingredients except water and cornstarch.
- Bring to a boil and simmer until vegetables are tender, about 10-15 minutes.
- Dissolve cornstarch in cold water and stir into hot salsa.
- Simmer for 5 more minutes.
- Ladle into hot sterilized jars.
- Process in a boiling water bath for 15 minutes.
- Serve with nachos or with your favorite Mexican dishes. This is also great over scrambled eggs or on hot dogs.

Yield: 14 pints — 14, 2-cup (500 mL) jars.

Note: *You can purée half of the tomatoes for a less chunky salsa. If you want a hotter salsa add more jalapeño peppers or pass the Tabasco when you open the jar. This can be used immediately.*

See photograph on the back cover.

Canned Apple Pie Filling

Great for pies or apple crisp or turnovers.

12 cups	peeled, cored and sliced apples	3 L
1 cup	water	250 mL
1 cup	sugar	250 mL
1 tbsp.	lemon juice	15 mL
½ tsp.	salt	2 mL
¾ cup	cold water	175 mL
½ cup	cornstarch	125 mL
1½ tsp.	cinnamon	7 mL

- In a large heavy pot, place sliced apples and water. Simmer over medium heat until apples are tender but not totally cooked (definitely not mushy), 5 minutes.
- Add sugar, lemon juice and salt.
- Bring to a boil and cook until sugar is dissolved.
- Combine cold water and cornstarch, mixing until well blended.
- Add cornstarch mixture to apple mixture and cook, stirring constantly, until thick and bubbly.
- Stir in cinnamon.
- Pour into hot sterilized quart (1 L) sealers.
- Seal and process in boiling water bath for 20 minutes.

Yield: 2 quarts (2 L), enough for 2 pies.

Hint: *When making pies with this filling, dot top with butter before placing top crust on pie.*

Variation: *Peaches may be used instead of apples. Increase cornstarch to ⅔ cup (150 mL).*

Apricot Jam

The flavor of this jam on fresh homemade bread is outstanding.

5 cups	sliced apricots (packed)	1.25 L
½ cup	water	125 mL
3⅓ cups	sugar	825 mL
1 tbsp.	lemon juice	15 mL

- Sterilize jars and place in a 225°F (107°C) oven to keep warm or in a boiling water bath.
- Combine apricots and water in a heavy Dutch oven. Over medium heat, bring to a boil; simmer for 10 minutes, stir occasionally. Mash with a potato masher.
- Add sugar and lemon juice. Turn heat to medium high.
- Boil, stirring frequently, for 25-30 minutes, or until of desired thickness.
- Pour into hot jars and process in a boiling water bath for 10 minutes.

Yield: 3 pints — 6 cups (1.5 mL).

Note: Make 1 batch at a time. Doubling causes scorching on the bottom of the pot due to a longer cooking time.

See photograph on the back cover.

Strawberry Jam

This jam is just bursting with flavor. It spreads nicely too!

12 cups	sliced strawberries	3 L
2 tbsp.	lemon juice	30 mL
8 cups	sugar	2 L
6 oz.	pkg. strawberry gelatin	170 g

- Wash jars in hot soapy water. Rinse. Place on a baking sheet, tops up, and keep warm in 225°F (107°C) oven. Jars will be nice and hot when ready to fill.
- Put all the berries into a very large heavy pot, and add lemon juice and sugar, stirring until well mixed.
- Bring to a boil over high heat, stirring constantly.
- Reduce to medium heat and boil for 30 minutes, stirring occasionally.
- Add strawberry gelatin and boil for 2 more minutes over medium heat.
- Remove from heat and skim. Pour into hot sterilized jars and seal.

Yield: 5 pints — 10 cups (2.5 L).

See photograph on the back cover.

Strawberry Rhubarb Sauce

Great on ice cream, pancakes or mixed with yogurt.

6 cups	sliced rhubarb	1.5 L
15 oz.	pkg. frozen sliced strawberries	425 mL
1 cup	sugar	250 mL

- Pour everything into a large kettle and bring to a boil over medium heat.
- Simmer until rhubarb is soft and starting to fall apart, sugar is dissolved and all is well blended and starting to thicken, about 10-15 minutes.
- Serve warm or cold.

Yield: 5 cups (1.25 L).

Note: *If using this sauce to flavor yogurt chill first. For a more tart sauce, reduce sugar.*

Hot Fudge Sauce

This recipe from my friends Dena, Teresa and Kathryn, is very popular with members of our church congregation in Drayton Valley.

3 cups	white sugar	750 mL
¾ cup	cocoa	175 mL
½ cup	flour	125 mL
3 cups	cold milk	750 mL
3 tbsp.	butter OR margarine	45 mL
2 tsp.	vanilla	10 mL

- In a large saucepan, combine sugar, cocoa and flour. Stir well.
- Add milk, butter and vanilla, mixing well.
- Bring to a boil over medium-high heat, stirring constantly for 3 minutes.
- Lower heat and cook until thick.
- Serve warm or cold over ice cream.
- Store in refrigerator.

Yield:. 1 quart (1 L) of sauce.

Note: *Not suitable for chocolate milk. If you prefer a thicker sauce, increase flour to ⅔ cup (150 mL).*

Chocolate Syrup

Don't be alarmed, this sauce thickens as it cools! My husband, a "chocoholic", created this recipe.

3 cups	sugar	750 mL
6 tbsp.	sifted cocoa	90 mL
1½ cups	corn syrup	375 mL
1½ cups	milk	300 mL
1 tsp.	vanilla, almond OR peppermint extract	5 mL

- In a large heavy saucepan, stir sugar and cocoa together.
- Stir in corn syrup and milk.
- Bring to a boil over medium-high heat, stirring constantly.
- Reduce heat and continue to boil for 6 minutes, stirring occasionally.
- Remove from heat and cool. Stir in vanilla. Skim off any foam on top.
- When cold, thin with small amounts of boiling water to desired thickness. Store in refrigerator.
- Serve over ice cream or add to hot or cold milk for a chocolate drink.

Yield: 1 quart (1 L) of syrup.

Homemade Sweetened Condensed Milk

Use in any recipe containing sweetened condensed milk.
You will achieve the same results at a lower cost.

¼ cup	regular margarine	60 mL
⅔ cup	white sugar	150 mL
1 cup	instant skim milk powder	250 mL
⅓ cup	hot water	75 mL

- Pour all ingredients into a blender. Blend until smooth and creamy.
- Pour into a covered jar or other container and refrigerate for 3 hours or overnight.
- Sugar dissolves and mixture thickens as it becomes cold.

Yield: 1⅓ cups (325 mL) OR 1 can of sweetened condensed milk.

Index

205

Share Flavors of Home with a friend

Order *Flavors of Home* at $16.95 per book plus $4.00 (total order) for shipping and handling.

Number of copies _____ x $16.95 = $ _____

Postage and handling _____ = $ _____ 4.00

Subtotal _____ = $ _____

In Canada add 7% GST _____(Subtotal x .07) = $ _____

Total enclosed _____ = $ _____

U.S. and international orders payable in U.S. funds./ Price is subject to change.

NAME: _____

STREET: _____

CITY: _____ PROV./STATE _____

COUNTRY _____ POSTAL CODE/ZIP _____

Please make cheque or money order payable to: **Palastair Enterprises**
P.O. Box 5082
Drayton Valley, Alberta
TOE OMO

For fund raising or volume purchases, contact **Palastair Enterprises** for volume rates.

Please allow 3-4 weeks for delivery

Share Flavors of Home with a friend

Order *Flavors of Home* at $16.95 per book plus $4.00 (total order) for shipping and handling.

Number of copies _____ x $16.95 = $ _____

Postage and handling _____ = $ _____ 4.00

Subtotal _____ = $ _____

In Canada add 7% GST _____(Subtotal x .07) = $ _____

Total enclosed _____ = $ _____

U.S. and international orders payable in U.S. funds./ Price is subject to change.

NAME: _____

STREET: _____

CITY: _____ PROV./STATE _____

COUNTRY _____ POSTAL CODE/ZIP _____

Please make cheque or money order payable to: **Palastair Enterprises**
P.O. Box 5082
Drayton Valley, Alberta
TOE OMO

For fund raising or volume purchases, contact **Palastair Enterprises** for volume rates.

Please allow 3-4 weeks for delivery